HOWARD FOSDICK

Computer
Basics for Librarians
and
Information
Scientists

with a foreword by F. WILFRID LANCASTER

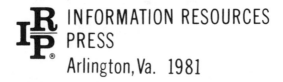 INFORMATION RESOURCES
PRESS
Arlington, Va. 1981

© 1981 by Information Resources Press, a division of Herner & Company.

Available from
Information Resources Press
1700 North Moore Street
Arlington, Virginia 22209

Library of Congress Catalog Card Number 81-80539
ISBN 0-87815-034-X

To my family

Contents

Foreword

There are several reasons why I am most happy to write a foreword to this book. First and foremost, the author was one of my students at the Graduate School of Library Science, University of Illinois, and it is personally rewarding to find a former student who remains industrious and productive and who is so clearly making a name for himself in the field of information science. I like to think I was able to make some small contribution to this success story.

A second reason is that I believe Fosdick has written a book that is very much needed. There are many introductory texts on computers and data processing. But there is no other text, as far as I am aware, that provides such a broad overview of this field, with an emphasis on the needs and interests of the library and information science community. He has kept library applications in mind throughout the text. By virtue of his training and recent experience, Fosdick is well qualified to undertake a work of this kind.

Moreover, I think he has been highly successful. He writes clearly and presents his material in a simple and straightforward manner that should be meaningful and understandable to the practicing librarian and to the student of library science. The book should be of great value to both categories of readers and should be suitable for use as a text in any course designed to introduce students to computers and their application in the library/information science environment.

F. Wilfrid Lancaster
Professor of Library Science
University of Illinois

Preface

For more than 15 years, libraries have been using computers in all aspects of library activity, including acquisitions, cataloging, circulation control, serials, and administrative data-processing functions. Simultaneously, entirely new forms of "libraries" have developed, represented by various information storage and retrieval systems that are based on computer technology. Developments in both of these areas have led to a demand for literature addressed to the general problems of library automation and to computer usage in library and information retrieval environments. Library administrators, library systems analysts, programmers, librarians, library science students, and others all require information in these areas. The resultant body of literature has developed a dual nature. Some books deal with library automation and are addressed to library professionals, while others might be classified under computer science. Works in the latter group may be technically oriented, demonstrating little effort by their authors to relate technical concepts and methodologies to an audience not conversant with detailed aspects of computer systems and programming.

This book is dedicated to bridging the gap between the two bodies of literature. It is not a work on library automation nor is it a technical treatise. Instead, it attempts to describe and analyze computing systems concepts in relation to forms that computer systems have taken in libraries.

A *computing system* may be defined as the totality of resources and knowledge required for the successful use of a computer. Many aspects of computing systems will be discussed in this book, ranging from hardware and software concepts to personnel and documentation requirements. In all cases, the purpose is the same: to introduce computing systems principles to persons concerned with libraries in comprehensible terms.

An effort has been made to concentrate on subjects of greatest relevance to library computing environments. The sections on storage considerations and programming languages, for example, stress issues of particular importance in library computing systems.

At the same time, special attention has been given to those topics commonly ignored in books dealing with library automation and information science. Discussions on operating systems and the internal methods of computer memory management, for example, usually are deferred by such works due to the technical nature of these subjects. The attitude adopted in this book is that persons in libraries, as intelligent computer users, should be familiar with technical computing principles such as multiprogramming and virtual storage. Librarians and other computer technology users can certainly understand these concepts when they are presented in a straightforward manner and are directly related to their own computing systems and concerns.

I would like to thank the following people for their constructive criticisms, help in refining the manuscript, or other "advice along the way": Dr. Karen Mackey, formerly Assistant Professor of Computer Science, Northern Illinois University, currently of Bell Laboratories, Naperville, Illinois; Dr. Andrew Torok, Assistant Professor, Dept. of Library Science, Northern Illinois University; Dr. Sylvia Faibisoff, Chairperson of the Dept. of Library Science, Northern Illinois University; Ms. Priscilla Polk, formerly Systems Programmer, Kane County Government Center, Geneva, Illinois; Ms. Theresa Goluszek, Programmer/Analyst, Digital Systems House, Batavia, Illinois; Mr. Hillis Griffin, Director, Technical Information Services, Argonne National Laboratory, Argonne, Illinois; Mr. Jim Knock, formerly Systems Analyst, Technical Information Services Division, Argonne National Laboratory, Argonne, Illinois; and Mr. Terrence Disz, of the Dept. of Computer Science, Northern Illinois University.

I would especially like to thank my father, Lee B. Fosdick, for his careful proofreading of the manuscript. And finally, I wish to express my gratitude to Dr. F. Wilfrid Lancaster, of the Graduate School of Library Science at the University of Illinois, for his reading of the manuscript and aid in securing its publication.

CHAPTER 1

Computing Systems Hardware

INTRODUCTORY CONCEPTS

Computing systems *hardware* is the physical equipment of a computing system, that is, the computer itself and attached devices, such as teletype terminals, disk drives, tape drives, card readers, printers, and other peripheral equipment that can be found in a computer operations room.

Although hardware refers to the physical manifestations of a computer system, its companion term, *software,* refers to an equally important aspect of that system—the programs that are run on the computer to perform the work required by the user.

To illustrate a few simple distinctions among hardware concepts, a diagram of a simplified computing system is presented in Figure 1.

The first distinction is between the *computer* itself and its various attached *input/output* (I/O) *devices.* The computer sometimes is referred to as the *central processor unit* (CPU), the *central processor,* or the *processor.* The CPU may be considered the "brain" of the computer system, but it always should be remembered that this brain is endowed with none of the creativity or capacity for original thought of its creators. Rather, the central processor can only execute instructions previously written for it by its "director," the *computer programmer.*

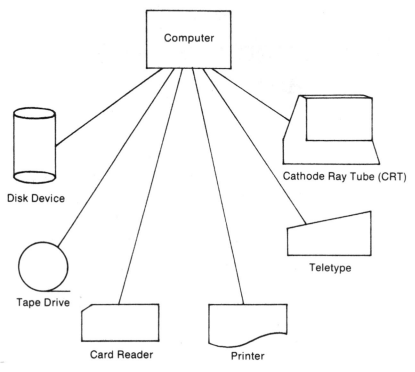

Figure 1 A SIMPLIFIED COMPUTING SYSTEM.

Input/output devices allow for various forms of contact between the computer and the outside world. In other words, they provide for communication with the computer. For example, a *card reader* reads data into the computer system from keypunched computer cards; a *printer* allows the processor to communicate the processing results back to human controllers. Other I/O devices include tape drives, teletypes, cathode ray tubes, disk drives, drums, data cells, and mass storage devices. *Tape drives* read and/or write on magnetic tapes, similar to those used on home tape recorders. *Teletypes* are keyboard devices, similar to electric typewriters, that allow for input to and output from a computer. *Cathode ray tubes* (CRTs) are like teletypes, except that CRTs have a television tube for data output or display. *Disk drives* consist of numerous flat platters, similar to those of a phonograph disk, but the platters of a disk contain magnetically encoded information. *Drums* are fast-rotating cylinders with data magnetically recorded on their surfaces. *Data cells* and *mass storage systems* are a class of devices that store large quantities of data through magnetization in one of several physical forms.

Almost any medium can be used as an input/output device for an electronic computer, including digital displays, panel lights, and graphic pen-plotters. An important aspect of the capability and utility of any computing system is the nature of its I/O devices. These will be discussed in greater detail in Chapter 3. The present discussion will focus on two aspects of I/O devices: input and/or output of data information to or from the CPU and data storage.

A disk allows for input/output to or from the computer, since information on the disk may be read by the CPU through the prompting of commands in a particular computer program. At the same time, the disk will be saving or storing large amounts of data on its surface. A printer also embodies the roles of both an input/output device and a storage medium. In the case of the printer, a program being executed on the CPU may give instructions to print out certain data, which is done through the printer or output device. This data may then be viewed as being stored on the paper on which it was printed; however, the data is not stored on the paper in a computer-readable or *machine-readable form*.

THE CPU

Figure 2 provides a more specific picture of the main components of a typical CPU. The *control unit* interprets instructions and directs the machine in executing the instructions. In this diagram, the control unit includes the computer's one or more timing devices or *clocks*, which are used in the synchronization of the computer's internal processes.

The *arithmetic/logical unit* is a term applied to that part of the CPU that is responsible for performing the operations indicated by many of the basic instructions that the computer can perform. These instructions include *arithmetic operations,* such as division, addition, subtraction, and multiplication, and *comparison operations,* by which the equality or inequality of specific data elements is determined.

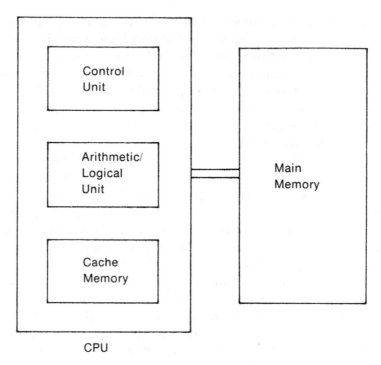

CPU

Figure 2   THE MAIN COMPONENTS OF A TYPICAL CPU.

Arithmetic and comparison instructions are fundamental to the function of the CPU as a whole, since a computer essentially is a symbol-manipulating machine. The computer is perceived as being capable of performing useful work because it manipulates symbols that are familiar to the user, for example, the digits 0 through 9 and the letters of the alphabet.

The *cache memory* is a small, temporary memory within the CPU; it is very fast, but very expensive. Its purpose is to speed up the operations of the CPU; that is, a computer with cache memory usually can execute instructions faster or perform better than the same model of computer without cache memory. Cache memory generally is not included in such basic CPU diagrams as shown in Figure 2. It is included here because it is not available in all computers, and it may be a significant factor of computer architecture affecting computer performance with which computer users should be familiar. Librarians particularly need to be aware that cache memory is available on only some minicomputers, yet that feature can aid minicomputer speed significantly when it is available, given current technology.

Registers

Although not specifically referred to in Figure 2, *registers* are important in relation to the operations and capabilities of the CPU. Registers are the tiny storage spaces in which the work actually done by the CPU is performed. For example, to add two numbers, the CPU may put the first number in register 1, the second number in register 2, then add the values in these two registers, putting the result into register 3. Registers are very fast devices for computation and comparison, and, although most CPUs can perform operations in other places within the computer, registers are the preferred place for actual work to be done.

The number of registers a CPU has is one of many important variables that describe its relative power. Large computers, such as the IBM Series 360 and Series 370, may have 16 registers. Many minicomputer CPUs may have eight or six or even only one register. Therefore, a processor with only a single register is likely to operate more slowly than one with many.

Memory

Main memory, core memory, core, primary memory, or *random access memory* (RAM) is the final component of Figure 2 to be discussed. In this figure, the computer memory is shown to the right of the CPU and is labelled "Main Memory."

The amount of main memory or core available traditionally has been a primary limiting factor in the development of computing systems. Core usually accounts for a large part of the expense of a computer system, and, often, the amount of core in a system is a limiting factor in how much and what kind of work that system can perform. Thus, determining how much main memory a computer has is very significant in gauging the capacity for work or relative "goodness" of a computing system.

Main memory is that area in which a computer program resides during its *execution,* or running. Some or all of the program's data may be kept in the main memory with the program. The key difference between main memory and that memory or storage provided by I/O devices is that core is randomly accessible by the movement of electrons only. It is electronic. Access to data stored on tape, for example, is not solely electronic, because physical movement may be involved as well—for example, the physical rotation of the tape. Thus, central to the definition of core memory is that it is purely electronic, accessed by the movement of electrons only. As will be pointed out in Chapter 4, core is usually many magnitudes faster for data access than I/O devices.

Figure 3 shows one physical form that main memory has taken in modern computers. Small magnetic rings, called *cores,* have a

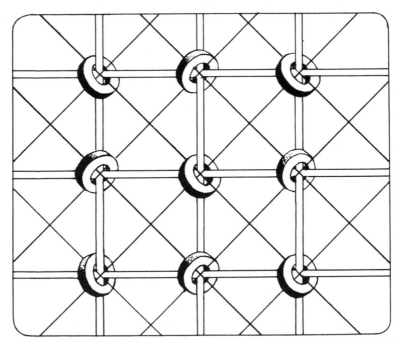

Figure 3 MAIN MEMORY IMPLEMENTED THROUGH CORE TECHNOLOGY.

number of wires passing through them, two of which are shown in this illustration. An electric current passing through one of the wires magnetizes and flips the core in one direction. Current passing through the other wire leaves the core magnetized in the opposite direction. Thus, there are two possible positions for any given core. This means that by magnetizing a core to a given position and leaving it that way, data or information is stored, which can later be sensed or "read."

Other physical forms of main memory, such as semiconductor memory, enjoy widespread use in today's electronic computers. But core was chosen for description because it directly relates to the next topic to be discussed: internal data representation in electronic computers.

INTERNAL DATA REPRESENTATION

The previous discussion explained that core memory consists of cores, magnetized in one of two directions. Although computer memory may appear in different physical forms, all follow the same basic principle of *binary digits* (or bits) for the encoding of information. The *bit* is the most fundamental unit of data representation, having one of two possible positions, usually referred to as + and − or, most often, as 0 and 1. Obviously, a single bit, in itself, does not contain very much information, since it has only two possible settings.

But a string of contiguous bits in computer memory can be used to express a more complex unit of information. For example, a *string* (contiguous group) of eight consecutive bits yields 2^8 or 256 possible settings, when it is assumed that each of the eight bits in the string has a uniquely meaningful position and setting in the string. Examples of such eight-bit strings are 10011001 and 10000011. This grouping of bits into consecutive strings of eight bits creates *bytes*. One important form of data representation in computers is to use bytes to express characters, digits, spaces, and punctuation marks. Since there are 256 possible unique bit strings that may make up a byte, a code of data representation based on this scheme will allow 256 different *characters,* or symbols, to be expressed internally. The Extended Binary Coded Decimal Interchange Code (EBCDIC) is based on these principles. Computers that use EBCDIC encoding of information are designed at the hardware level so that bits are naturally grouped by the computer into groups of eight and so that bytes may be easily represented and manipulated.

An alternative code for representing letters of the alphabet, digits, and other symbols is the American Standard Code for Information Interchange (ASCII), which uses seven-bit strings to represent individual symbols. There are 2^7 or 128 possible characters that may be represented by the ASCII code.

It should be mentioned that there are other codes and formats for internal character representation used in computers, for example, a six-bit form of the ASCII code. Another six-bit code is *binary coded decimal* representation, or BCD. But seven-bit ASCII and, particularly, EBCDIC are by far the most common and, therefore, are considered standards. Appendix A provides tables showing how symbols are represented in these two encoding schemes.

To give an example of data encoding, the word HOUSE has five characters and would require five bytes to be represented in the EBCDIC code (and 5 × 8 or 40 bits). ASCII would require only 5 × 7 or 35 bits to encode the same word, because it uses only seven bits to express each English letter. Note that the words THE HOUSE would require four (not three) extra bytes in either code, since the space between the words is itself a symbol requiring a byte for storage. As is evident, it takes a byte to represent any given character in computer memory. *Character,* in this sense, refers to digits, spaces, and punctuation marks, as well as letters of the alphabet.

There are no inherent advantages to using either of these bit encoding schemes. On one hand, ASCII saves one bit of space for any character represented.[1] In a particular instance of library use, however, EBCDIC presents an advantage: This encoding scheme, with its greater number of possible symbol representations, has a larger number of "free" bit combinations not yet used for

---

[1]Most seven-bit ASCII computers, however, actually store each seven-bit character within an eight-bit byte.

representing any symbols. In library programming, it is possible to use these unassigned bit combinations for purposes defined by the programmer. EBCDIC offers many more usable bit-string combinations for libraries encoding foreign-language material with characters not currently included in either ASCII or EBCDIC codes. Normally, it is not important whether a computer operates internally in ASCII or EBCDIC. But when libraries wish to use symbols not currently in the code, such as those in foreign languages, EBCDIC may offer more room for such "special characters."

When information is received that is coded in the opposite format from that which the computer uses, the incoming data must be converted to the local format. For example, the Machine Readable Cataloging (MARC) tapes are in ASCII format. If an in-house computer operates in EBCDIC, the MARC tapes must be converted to EBCDIC code, which can be accomplished through the running of a translation program written specifically for this purpose. Writing the program is well within the capabilities of the average programmer, but running it may require a significant amount of processing time.

Both ASCII- and EBCDIC-based computers have a number of other important coding schemes used for numerical computations: *Packed* or *decimal arithmetic, floating point,* and *fixed point* are some of these methods. The most important internal representation for numbers, however, is in base two; that is, since computer memory physically works with *binary* digits, base two arithmetic is highly convenient and appropriate. Table 1 illustrates counting from 1 to 16 in what is usually referred to as *binary mathematics,* or *binary.*

Figure 4 depicts the general process of how a number might be read into an EBCDIC-based computer, processed, and printed out again. The number to be input, here 12, has been punched on a computer or Hollerith[2] card through the use of a keypunch machine. The computer program that reads this card converts the number to its binary equivalent. After some unspecified processing occurs, an answer of 1110 (base two) is produced and then is printed. The computer program converts this binary number to its equivalent in terms of the EBCDIC coding scheme. Since the

---

[2]Punched computer cards are sometimes referred to as "Hollerith cards." Herman Hollerith invented the punched card concept while working for the United States Bureau of the Census in the 1880s.

TABLE 1   Binary Numbers and Their Decimal Equivalents

Counting in Base Two (Binary)	Decimal Equivalent
1	1
10	2
11	3
100	4
101	5
110	6
111	7
1000	8
1001	9
1010	10
1011	11
1100	12
1101	13
1110	14
1111	15
10000	16

number is 14, it takes two EBCDIC bytes to describe it, one for each character or digit involved. With the number now in EBCDIC, it may be printed as 14. Important points in this example include:

1. The computer often performs input and output operations, such as reading and printing a number, in its "native" code of either ASCII or EBCDIC.

2. EBCDIC or ASCII representation of numbers may be converted to and from their respective binary equivalents, and programmers have the means to do this within their programs. Note that binary math is only a scheme for expressing numbers. Characters, letters of the alphabet, and so on, can only be left in EBCDIC or ASCII.

3. Numbers usually may be stored more efficiently in computer memory and manipulated in the binary system than in coding schemes like EBCDIC or ASCII, which is why programmers go through the process of the conversions shown in Figure 4.

These points lead directly to some important considerations for the library programming environment. The following bibliographic citation has digits in the title, the year, and the page numbers:

Heinrich, M. *Germany Since 1919.* Dusseldorf: Barenreiter Press, 1972, pp. 33–84.

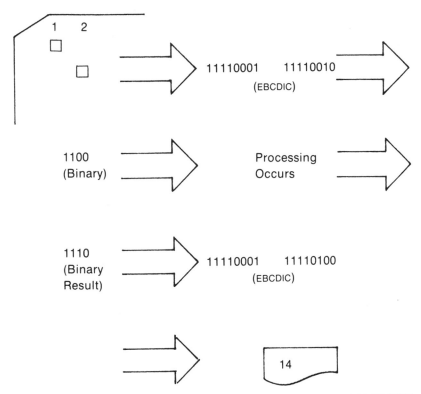

Figure 4   NUMBER CONVERSIONS REQUIRED DURING COMPUTER PROCESSING.

None of the digits, however, will be used in numeric computations; that is, in all probability, the user does not wish to add,
divide, or otherwise compute with the years or the page numbers.
Instead, only storage, retrieval, and manipulation of the bibliographic citation as a whole are desired. Thus, the "numbers" in
this reference would best be stored in the same data format as the
rest of the record (either EBCDIC or ASCII, since characters cannot be
stored as binary numbers). Treating digits the same as other
characters, such as letters of the alphabet, punctuation marks, and
spaces, leads to their being referred to as *character digits* or *character-
format numbers*. Note that for a number like 1972, it will take four
characters × 8 bits/character, or 32 bits, to express the number in
EBCDIC, versus only 11 bits to represent the same number in binary
or base two.

Although it is somewhat more efficient to express digits as binary numbers, library programming tends to view digits as character-format data. The reason for this and its implications are important and will be discussed in greater detail in Chapter 8 on library software needs. The point here is that digits may be considered and represented internally as either computational quantities or character-format data, similar to letters of the alphabet.

Today's marketplace tends to use EBCDIC more widely in large computers, often referred to as *mainframes*. Frequently, ASCII is the code used in *minicomputers* and the still smaller *microcomputers*.

Computer size is further reflected through hardware representations of data in the size of the data units commonly manipulated. With mainframes, bytes may be conveniently manipulated in groups of four—four bytes being equivalent to one *word*. Word size for minicomputers is usually two bytes, which would be 16 bits for most computers. Microcomputers were distinguished by a word size corresponding to a single byte. It is important to investigate both the word size and the character code when comparing computer systems. When a computer salesman comes into the library offering a "40,000-word system," is this a 40,000-, 80,000-, or 160,000-byte computer? And what is the size of a byte? Unfortunately, computer terminology is not always standardized or accurate in this area.

SUMMARY

This chapter has introduced the basic hardware components of modern digital computers, as well as the functions of these components. To the extent that they are involved in the evaluation (and purchase or rental) of computer equipment, librarians need to be familiar with terminology relating to hardware.

Methods for internally representing data within computer systems are directly based on the fundamental unit of memory the hardware can represent—the bit. The two major methods of data representation were discussed. Most data in the library programming environment is stored and manipulated in character-format representations. This fact distinguishes libraries from many other computer users and leads directly to the rather different nature of library software requirements. The exact nature of library programming will be further defined in Chapter 8.

CHAPTER 2

Personnel

The preceding chapter on common configurations of computing systems hardware naturally leads to a discussion of the social organization necessary to complement a computing system's hardware. Who, in fact, runs the equipment, schedules valuable computer time, services the system hardware, and writes the programs that direct the processor? The answer to all of these questions is an entire organization of personnel concerned specifically with the computer system at the particular institution under consideration.

At large computer installations, the individuals operating a mainframe have position titles and job functions that are fairly specific and well defined. In this chapter, the job responsibilities at a large *shop* are discussed, in order to clearly detail the personnel functions required at any installation.

Library programming shops, of course, will tend to be much smaller than those businesses employing 30, or 50, or even more than 100 persons in their computing personnel divisions. But a key factor is that any programming organization must fulfill certain functions in order to successfully operate a computer. In large business organizations, these functions may be defined by the delegation of an individual or many individuals to each function. Discussing these functions in terms of the large organization may aid in delineating their exact natures, but it must be remembered that even small computer users, such as libraries, must perform the functions to be discussed. The manner in which libraries may do this will be analyzed later in this chapter.

PROGRAMMERS

In a large company using a computer, the staff of *programmers* may perform many related functions. The basic responsibility of the staff is to design, write, modify, enhance, test, and maintain computer programs. A *program* is a logical methodology for performing work that is written in a particular computer language. As mentioned earlier, the central processor can do work only by executing a computer program; otherwise, the computer sits idle.

Programmers, then, can take a well-defined problem, conceptualize and logically analyze it in terms of how the computer can work on the problem, and write a solution in a language that the computer can understand. After writing the program, programmers must extensively test or *debug* it. Such testing is essential to ensure that the program does indeed do what it was written to do. Very often the program will be only a part of a system of interacting programs designed to achieve some larger objective. When this is the case, test time, sometimes called *systems testing,* can consume the major portion of the time spent on producing the program. A common maxim is that the amount of time spent in producing a finished and working program increases exponentially as a function of the complexity of the program (and the system of which it is a part, if any).

A surprising aspect of programming to most persons unfamiliar with its nature is that the largest portion of a programmer's time is spent modifying, enhancing, and maintaining existing programs. Programmers usually refer to this work as *maintenance.* At any given shop, perhaps 90 percent of programmer time is spent on maintenance.

Why is maintenance such a time-consuming task? The modifications in the performance of a program are fairly common. Often, such changes in a program's purpose or function are requested immediately upon completion of the program. These changes may be due either to the programmer's incorrect perception of what was desired of the program, or to a feeling on the part of the originator of the program request that the program does not fit the problem. The latter may be caused by the originator's realization that the *output* (printed report) requested of the program was not actually what was needed. Or it may be a case of misrepresenting the problem to the programmer. In any case, there are many reasons for initial modifications to a "completed" program; these will be discussed further when the job of the systems analyst is described. For now, note that miscommunication concerning program purposes and associated modifications of original programs are costly and common events in any programming environment.

The bulk of maintenance performed by programmers involves programs that appear to have been working satisfactorily and then mysteriously break down for unknown reasons. Sometimes this is the result of faulty logic in the program—the programmer's responsibility. At other times, unanticipated "cases" or situations occur in the program. For example, suppose a library payroll program has worked successfully for two years. One day it fails, halting after printing the third paycheck. It is discovered that data input for the fourth employee shows a total of zero hours worked for that week and that the program was not written properly to handle this situation. This may be the result of a programmer logic error or failure of the programmer to consider this case and provide for it in the program logic, a programmer misunderstanding concerning the possibility that this situation would ever occur, or incorrect data entry. Perhaps it had been previously agreed never to enter a weekly record of zero hours worked, but a new employee in data entry did not know this.

As another example, consider an acquisitions program that uses six bytes for storing an acquisition date for a bibliographic item. Since one byte means one symbol can be stored, the six bytes may be used to save the acquisitions date in this manner: MMDDYY, where M stands for the month, D for the day, and Y for the year (e.g., Christmas 1980 would be 122580). One day, namely the first day in the year 2000, many of the programs using this acquisition date will break down. By looking at the date, 010100, the reason becomes clear. The two digits representing the year are insufficient to distinguish the year 1900 from the year 2000. The existing programs may have required this distinction in order to run properly.

A few reasons why programs fail have been briefly detailed,

and the most critical fact is that maintenance programming fills most of the working time of the majority of programmers. Before continuing the discussion of this crucial issue relative to the position of systems analysts, a key distinction must be made between *applications* and *systems* programmers.

The *user* of an applications programmer can be virtually any employee in an organization requesting a program(s) to perform work of direct use to that user. Applications programmers are involved with computer programs that print reports or other end products of direct benefit to their users. In a library, for example, applications programmers may serve such users as the head of the circulation department, requesting a program to generate and analyze circulation statistics; the cataloging department, requesting programs to print catalog cards; and the personnel division, requesting a program to search the employee record files to find a reference librarian to fill a new vacancy in the chemistry branch library.

Systems programmers, on the other hand, are involved only with *systems programming*. They program to make modifications in the computer system itself, writing highly technical internal programs to extend or change the software of the computing system. The users of systems programmers are the applications programmers and other personnel of the computing center. Systems programmers normally do not interact with noncomputer personnel of the company or library for which they work.

It is the applications programmers who are commonly referred to as "computer programmers." The systems programmers are there, however, writing necessary internal programs and modifications to keep the computer system "up" and running. Their job will be more completely explained in Chapter 5 on the *operating system*. For the present time, it is important to note that the distinction made between these two types of programmers almost invariably is found in large computer-using organizations.

The background, training, and abilities of these two groups of programmers are different. Systems programmers have more specialized training than do applications programmers. Similar gradations of experience or seniority are found among both, often following the progression of programmer trainee, junior programmer, programmer, senior programmer, and lead programmer.

SYSTEMS ANALYSTS

In the preceding discussion, it was stated that applications programmers interact with users who are not members of the computer staff. In a large organization, it is rarely true that programmers deal directly with their users. Instead, *systems analysts* usually interface between the two groups. The systems analyst, or analyst, discusses with the user the nature of the program request and attempts to create the precise problem definition required to program a solution. In addition to formulating a problem definition, the systems analyst must translate the problem statement into the technical statement of how the computer can solve it. Often, this involves conferring with programmers, describing the problem to them in terms they can understand, and giving them a tentative solution or at least a technical problem statement to follow. Systems analysts always must consider the nonprogramming technical aspects of the problem, for example, hardware and software requirements, storage mediums and needs, costs, manpower, time considerations, project duration, and many other factors.

The analyst's job may be considered in three general aspects. First, communication is involved, both with the originator (or user) of a program request and with the programming staff. Second, in analyzing the problem and determining how to solve it, the analyst must consider the "systems planning" factors already cited. And, third, programming needs must be translated into a proper and feasible technological approach.

When the need for maintenance programming was discussed, it was noted that the analyst holds a key position in the process of translating a programming request into a working solution. Communication is of the utmost importance, and it is largely the analyst's job to ensure accurate and full communication between users, who may know little about computing, and programmers, who may know nothing of the user's true orientation and needs.

Obviously, it would be most beneficial to have analysts with backgrounds in both the business of the organization and in programming. Companies have difficulty, however, in hiring such well-qualified people as analysts. Most large organizations eventually collect a staff of analysts who are predominantly user oriented or who have fundamentally computer/technical backgrounds.

One further note should be made concerning systems analysts. In some corporations, they are on an equal level in the company hierarchy with programmers, performing the defined functions. In other organizations, they may be indirect supervisors of the programmers, also performing some of the managerial functions involved in running a data-processing center.

OPERATIONS

Operations personnel are those employees who take care of the physical needs of the computer. Computer *operators* must "bring up," start, or *IPL*[1] the system if it is not currently running. They must also service the devices, that is, fill the card reader with the proper cards, keep the printer supplied with paper, and separate the programs or *jobs* from one another after they have been output from the computer through the printer(s).

Operators also normally "start" jobs to be run by the system. Most installations have a *run book* describing when and how operators are supposed to submit specific jobs to the computer system.

A crucial part of the operator's job is communication with the controlling program of the computer system—called the *operating system*—through the *systems console*. The systems console is a particular teletype or CRT dedicated solely to communication between the operating system and the operators. Through the console, the operator may set up and start a given program's execution. The console may be used by the program to communicate error conditions to the operator. For instance, a program might check to make certain that a particular dataset or file of information is available. If not, it could output a console message to the operator that it could not properly function due to the lack of the dataset. The operator could then take appropriate corrective action. The

---

[1] *IPL* is "Initial Program Loading." In computer terminology, "to IPL the system" is "to start the system." Programmers commonly speak of "IPLing the system."

console, therefore, generally is used to inform operations personnel either that particular events have occurred or that errors have occurred requiring human intervention. The systems console was not discussed earlier due to its rather special nature. Any moderate to large computing system has a systems console, which the operators generally administer.

Computer operators, then, may handle many of the tasks involved in actually running programs. It should be mentioned that they usually have a vocational background, whereas programmers and systems analysts normally have degrees ranging from the junior college level through graduate school.

DATA ENTRY

Data entry into the computer system is performed by clerical personnel using one of three major methods: keypunching, key-to-tape, or key-to-disk.

Keypunching involves punching data onto computer cards for subsequent data entry. The cards usually are discarded after the information has been stored in internal computer files.

In *key-to-tape* data entry, data is typed directly on computer tape, which subsequently may be read via the computer's tape drives. This method is currently an attractive, although somewhat more expensive, alternative to traditional keypunched cards. Note that "cards" are not wasted, as corrections can be typed directly on the tape.

Key-to-disk entry is the newest and most effective variety of data entry. It is also the most convenient in several respects. Key-to-disk data-entry personnel normally use CRTs that are connected directly to the computer. They interact with either data-entry or *text editor* programs, which will be discussed in subsequent chapters on computer software. Basically, these computer programs interact with or respond to the person entering the data and allow for greater accuracy and ease of entry. The accuracy of data entered is crucial, because, once incorrect data is entered into the system, any subsequent use or reporting of that data (as in any report program) will result in further inaccuracies. This important topic of data accuracy is discussed later in this chapter. At this point, it should be emphasized that the key-to-disk method enhances accuracy in data entry through the use of computer programs prepared especially for this purpose. Also, a fact not often mentioned is that most typists find that their typing speed is faster with CRT keyboards. This is no small factor when a library may be entering many hundreds of bibliographic records daily.

Concluding the remarks on data entry, it might be pointed out that many volumes have been written on various aspects of data-entry methodologies and data conversion projects. The selective annotated bibliography at the end of this book lists some of these for further reference.

DATA-CONTROL CLERK

Most data-processing installations have one or more data-control clerks, whose job it is to verify the accuracy of the computer system's data input and output.

The data-control clerks' responsibilities concerning input data to the system vary widely according to the nature and types of processing done at the installation. When users of the program supply their own data, the data-control personnel will check it to be certain that it matches the type of data its associated program will be expecting.

On the output side, the data-control clerks will visually check report output for some predetermined signs of accurate program execution. In a business situation, for example, data control probably would want to check to ensure that the payroll program did not accidentally write a weekly salary check of $1 million. In a library, a common example would be to check that the results of a selective dissemination of information (SDI) program look reasonable. "Did we really mean to print out that list of juvenile fiction titles for the microbiological researchers?" Very elementary and quick sight-checking by data control can catch such errors before they become public commentary on the library's new computer system.

COMPUTER DATA CONTROL

The significance of data control has been discussed briefly, as well as the importance of admitting only accurate information into the storage files of the computing system. Computer programs can aid personnel involved in data control by the following methods. These error-checking programs are called *input-edit* programs.

First, a program can check a specific data element or *field* for *reasonableness*. For instance, a program might easily check the date of publication in a bibliographic citation. If the year is prior to 1450, an obvious error can be detected. Or to refer again to the example of the $1 million paycheck, the program might easily have recognized this amount as unreasonable.

Input-edit programs can also detect errors of *data type*. If a book's publication date were not digits, or if the author's name were numeric, an input-edit program would be able to assist data-control personnel in finding the mistake.

Completeness may also be checked by a computer program. A missing field will be read into the computer memory as all EBCDIC (or ASCII) space characters, and this is readily distinguished from the alphabetic or numeric data item that the program expected to read.

Finally, *check digits* may be used in assigning valid patron identification numbers. A check digit is a number selected and attached to an existing number so that certain mathematical manipulations of the entire number always will produce certain predictable results. Social security numbers incorporate check digits.

These are the major methodologies for ensuring data accuracy through input-edit computer programs. Good programmers and systems analysts will be certain to incorporate as many of these accuracy checks as possible into the programs they design and write. Together with skilled data-control clerks, such programming will go a long way toward rendering the data actually stored in the computer's files as accurate as possible. It is paramount, however, that neither the operator nor the machine aspect of data control be slighted on the assumption that one will suffice for the other.

LIBRARY COMPUTER PERSONNEL

Earlier in this chapter, the kinds of job positions and personnel responsibilities that are typically encountered in the computer services division or department of moderate to large businesses were described. In relating this corporate data-processing structure to libraries, the often-encountered distinction between libraries "owning" their own systems and those sharing their computer systems with some other organization(s) is highly pertinent. The literature on library automation commonly refers to these as *dedicated* versus *shared* computing systems. In the former situation, the library has total managerial control and responsibility for its computer system. In the latter case, the library may be sharing its computer with another institution, and this other institution is most often the parent organization. For example, a public library may share use of a computer with a city or county government. An academic library might be one of several organizational users of the university computer system. In either case, the total personnel responsibilities and structure are apt to be very different for the library with shared computer use versus the library that has its own dedicated system.

The shared computer situation connotes that the library is not the controlling or administrative organization for the computer installation. This leads directly to an associated fact—that the parent organization is frequently in charge of and responsible for personnel fulfilling those functional needs common to all user groups. Operations personnel, most systems-programming personnel, managerial positions relating directly to the operation of the installation, certain managerial/systems analyst jobs, and manual data control are likely to be the responsibility of the larger organization. Data-entry personnel may be centralized and, therefore, not under library administrative control. There are certainly many different patterns in such cases, but it is safe to assume that, in most situations of shared-computer use, the library retains its own data-processing staff. This group fulfills the functions of applications programmers and library systems analysts. The concept underlying the library's retention of its own dedicated programmer/analyst staff is that this staff will be more competent to meet library programming project needs.

Many of the aforementioned distinctions and comments referring to business data-processing employees also apply to libraries. In fact, there is background conflict between those programmers and analysts having primary library training and orientation and those computer professionals having no formal training or particular understanding of libraries and their needs. Unfortunately, C. P. Snow's thesis of the "two cultures"[2] finds fewer fields of more profound application than libraries. The lack of communication and understanding between the disciplines of library science and computer science is severe. Few persons have a meaningful background in both.

The solution to this situation, in practice, has been that libraries hire individuals for their data-processing staffs with backgrounds in library or computer science, but not both. Communication problems between the two groups therefore multiply, the only remedy being on-the-job training.

Graduate schools of library science have responded to the situation by rapidly expanding their curricula in the areas of library automation and information science. But most of these course offerings might best be labelled "computer familiarization" courses because of the degree of programming knowledge that students receive from such courses. It is rare to find a library school graduate who is capable of serious applications programming and is also acquainted with modern programming practices.

Another point relating to the business personnel positions examined earlier is that library computer personnel often fulfill responsibilities delegated to more than one employee in the business computer installation. Combining job duties into a single position is a response to the size of data-processing departments and is most significant with the smaller technical staff encountered in the shared-computer library environment. Library position titles sometimes reflect this occurrence, as in "programmer/analyst" and "library systems analyst." Library staffs may not be large enough to warrant analysts interceding between the

[2]Snow, C. P. *Two Cultures.* Cambridge, Mass., University Press, 1964.

applications programmers and their users. For example, a common situation occurs when the senior data-processing staff member performs many duties corresponding to those of the business systems analyst.

Due to this phenomenon of combining related functions into a particular library computer position, library administrators might want to analyze carefully the discrete responsibilities associated with a given position. In the case of the programmer/analyst, administrators should endeavor to see that these individuals as analysts have a definite orientation towards and feeling for the tasks of the library as an institution. The purpose of the data-processing staff is to further the needs of the library as a whole. Sometimes the administrative staff gives insufficient attention to the analyst functions of the programmer/analyst. Do the analysts attend library automation conferences and meetings to keep abreast of developments at other libraries?

On the other hand, the programmer/analyst must either be a competent programmer and technician or be trained to competency. Library administrators must recognize the rapid advances occurring in computer technology and methodologies. Are the programmers and analysts familiar with techniques like top-down design and structured programming? What about hardware advances in chip technology and CRTs? Continuing education is a proven way of keeping programmers and analysts up-to-date in technical areas.

Analysis of library employee functions in terms of business data-processing personnel structures also may point out deficiencies in the library data-processing organization. Some library staffs either lack a data-control clerk or use methods of data control abandoned by businesses as being obsolete. For instance, the data entered by one clerk in data entry always should be checked by another person—not the same clerk who originally entered the data.

An example of a library system lacking such data control is the Ohio College Library Center (OCLC). Here, proper data control is thwarted by the fact that this computing system is involved with input data from a large number of disparate libraries. The sort of central data-control function the individual library should embody simply is not enforceable by OCLC, given the organizational realities of its multiuser system.

To address the topic of the library owning or leasing its own computer system, the most readily apparent and important point is that the library must now employ a complete staff of computer professionals. This staff must be capable of fulfilling those functions previously discussed and will, therefore, correspond to the staffs encountered in many moderate-size business computer installations. This also means that the library will have the sometimes unpleasant responsibilities involved in the hardware and software maintenance of the computer system. On the hardware level, contracting for support and maintenance will be the library's most productive option, similar to most organizations that are not large enough to hire their own electronics technicians.

The software problem is one that is sometimes not sufficiently appreciated by library administrators planning a library computing system along these lines. Systems programmers, particularly competent ones, are hard to find and harder to keep once they are found. The systems-programming responsibility, as noted previously, is a discrete function separate from applications programming. If the systems-programming function is not adequately or properly fulfilled, it is not likely that the applications programmers will somehow be able to "fill the gap." The alternatives will be narrowed to expensive consulting services or extensive "down" (nonrunning) time. Naively or optimistically expecting applications programmers to perform systems programming will not be a successful administrative choice.

Library administrators involved in hiring their own computer staff should be certain to survey the market for computer professionals. Prominent computer industry newspapers such as *Computerworld* and *Information Systems News* can provide a quick and accurate idea of the general nature of this market. Journals such as *Datamation* and *Infosystems* also carry advertisements and articles that librarians responsible for hiring computer personnel can examine.

Counterbalancing the responsibilities and expense involved in a library having its own dedicated computing system and staff is the total administrative control the library has over its data-processing functions. The central concept here is that the computer department of the library exists to serve the needs and further the organizational goals of the library. Library administrative control in the dedicated-system model ensures that this will be true. Cases where the controlling organization changed library plans or altered library priority versus other computer-system users sometimes have led to "the tail wagging the dog" for library shared-system users. As these administrative advantages, inherent in the dedicated-system approach, have been discussed widely in library administrative literature, they will not be commented upon here.

SUMMARY

This chapter has described business employee organization in relation to moderate- to large-size computer systems. The generalized personnel structure has evolved over the past two decades as a response to the challenge of developing effective personnel systems for computer-support divisions. Libraries are not always required to fulfill the same range and variety of functions faced by commercial data-processing users. For example, libraries are assumed to have their own administrative/managerial structures, so these have not been discussed in relation to businesses. But comparing library computer staffs and employee functions with organizational methods proved valid among large and successful computer-using corporations may indeed prove fruitful for library administrators. In any case, librarians and administrators certainly should be aware of the ways in which their computer staffs reflect and differ from the common organizational forms found elsewhere.

CHAPTER 3

System Storage Considerations

In the first chapter, a variety of input/output devices such as tapes, disks, teletypes, and CRTs were briefly considered. In this chapter and Chapter 4, the general characteristics of system storage methods, their requirements, and the ways in which particular forms of computer storage may be used to meet these requirements will be discussed. Before approaching these topics, it is appropriate to mention why storage devices are so important to consider in library computer use.

In library computer systems, the computer commonly provides services such as library circulation control, on-line cataloging-aid systems, and, sometimes, on-line "card catalogs." A common denominator among the cataloging systems is that the basic unit of information is the bibliographic citation, or book or journal record. In both instances, the number of records to be stored is quite large. The on-line catalog is a complete inventory of every bibliographic item the library owns; in the on-line circulation system, the data stored in the computer consists either of the items currently borrowed or of a complete inventory of all items the library holds. In either case, whenever libraries are involved in storing data representing a large part of their collections in machine-readable or computer-accessible form, the computer storage requirement will be large. Compared to a business or corporate computer center employing an equivalent number of people, library storage needs can be enormous.

Since libraries often have large storage needs, they may be considered storage-intensive computing systems. The power of the local CPU may be only moderate, but the computer tape ''libraries'' or system disk storage capacity and costs may be comparatively great.

For these reasons, librarians and administrators must be well aware of the peculiarities, advantages, and disadvantages of particular computer storage mediums. They must be able to recognize which storage mediums are appropriate for which purposes and to mix and match storage devices in thoughtfully designed system configurations. Finally, they must be familiar with specific device characteristics and capacities and must understand the various methods for storing records on a given device. The library may require a significant investment in large-capacity disk drives; therefore, efficient disk use is important.

This chapter will investigate specific aspects of computer storage after a brief review of input/output devices. These devices were considered in two respects, as man/machine communication devices and as a medium for computer storage of information. Punched paper tape, for example, may be either read from or written on as it goes through a paper tape I/O device. Then it might be stored and, later, read and used to communicate data to the computer.

This process points out another useful distinction, namely, data storage that is on-line versus that which is not. If the paper tape roll is on the reader, so that a program being executed could read data from the tape at any time, the data is said to be *on-line*. Taking the paper tape off the reader, rolling it up, and placing it in a desk drawer renders it inaccessible to the computer. Without human intervention to place the paper tape back on the reader, it is not available to any computer program and is thus *off-line*. An important point to remember is that it costs much more to keep the data on-line, since a paper-tape reader must be used for this task. Due to the greater costs of on-line data, this chapter will focus on issues particularly pertinent to this topic.

DEVICE CHARACTERISTICS

What are significant storage device characteristics? Many relate to those distinctions just made. Is a device primarily oriented towards input and/or output of data, storage functions, or both? Is data portable and storable off-line, or must it be kept on-line? Once on-line, how rapidly can the data be *accessed* or read by a program? Device characteristics are so numerous, and often are so dependent on the user's viewpoint on which are the most important, that they are difficult to evaluate objectively. The paper tape used in the example was considered an awkward and obsolete storage and input/output medium in the late 1960s. In the mid-1970s, however, its slow speed mattered little to many enthusiastic microcomputer owners who appreciated its portability and low cost.

One common way of viewing on-line data storage devices is in terms of "memory hierarchies." This concept relates the key characteristics of storage capacity, relative cost per byte stored, and access speed by a program (*access time*), as shown in Figure 5. For storage mediums commonly encountered, a direct relationship exists between cost per byte of data stored and faster access time. At the same time, these two factors can be plotted inversely to the characteristic of greater storage capacity. There are certain trade-offs in choosing between particular devices. Notice the inclusion of main memory and cache memory in Figure 5. These are certainly forms of computer data storage, although, since they are solely electronically accessed, they do not meet the definition of input/output devices given in Chapter 1.

At this point, it might be wise to backtrack a bit and ask the question: What typically is stored in a computer system? Obviously, in order to execute any given program, the program must exist within the system's storage space in machine-readable form. In addition to programs that are written, certain software that is purchased with the computer also must be in the memory.

The other category of information stored is data for the executing program to work with, such as bibliographic citation information or serials acquisition information. In fact, at any moment in a computer system, there is a mass of data on-line that is not being used by the program immediately executing.

The basic unit of stored information may be called a *record* or *logical record*. A logical record, for example, might be all of the information concerning a given journal article, or it could be the

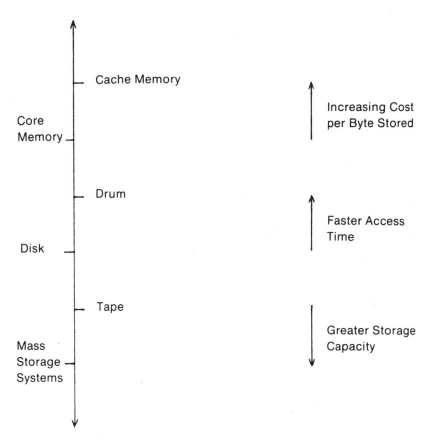

Figure 5 MEMORY HIERARCHIES.

collection of data found on a catalog card. The basic concept is that a typical record consists of logically related data elements commonly called *fields*. A group of all of the logical records of a particular type is a *file* or a *dataset*. In most storage mediums, records within a file are usually stored in contiguous spaces.

RECORD FORMATS

Logical records can be diagrammed as shown in Figures 6 and 7. These illustrations of an individual record, or a *record layout*, are

Field Names	Author ·	Title	Place of Publication	Publisher	Date	Purchase Price
Lengths (in bytes)	20	40	10	10	4	5

Figure 6   A LOGICAL BOOK RECORD.

possible because each field is expected to have a predictable length. When each record in a file has a given length, it is called a *fixed-length record*. Every fixed-length record outlined in Figures 6 and 7 would have the exact same format, the same fields occupying the same relative byte positions within the record. In Figure 7, for example, it is established that the patron ID field begins in position 1 of the record and has a length of six bytes; that the *patron name* field begins in relative record position 7 and continues for a total field length of 30 bytes, and so on. Thus, to read and manipulate this data, a computer program knows the exact location and type of data in each logical record, since the programmer was given this record layout from which to design a specific program. Note that computer programs often follow a cycle of reading in a single logical record, processing that record, writing out processing results, reading in the next record, processing that record and printing out its results, and so on, until there are no further records to be read and processed. This simple and straight-

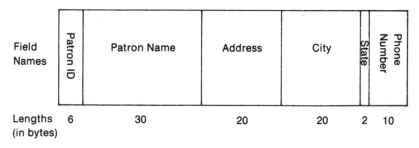

Field Names	Patron ID	Patron Name	Address	City	State	Phone Number
Lengths (in bytes)	6	30	20	20	2	10

Figure 7   A LOGICAL RECORD ABOUT A LIBRARY PATRON.

forward pattern of program logic often is used to process all the logical records of a given file or dataset.

What happens in a record layout when a given field is shorter than its designated record layout length? For example, in Figure 6, the length of the *author* field is 20 characters. Obviously, many bibliographic items might have an author whose name is only 10 or 15 characters long. Here, the author's name will be padded or extended on the right with "blanks" to render it exactly 20 characters long. This procedure is followed in creating fixed-length records so that each record is the same length and its fields occupy the same relative character positions within the record. Such fields are called *left-justified*. Numeric fields are extended to some predefined length by preceding them by an appropriate number of zeros, referred to as *right-justification*.

In Figure 6, if the *purchase price* of a given logical record was only $12.00 (expressed in the record in digits as 1200), then the field information is four characters long. But the fixed-length record format of Figure 6 defines a purchase price field of five digits. Making the number 01200 renders it the proper length. Notice that extending the number on the right, as in 12000, will not work, because it alters the number's value. This, then, is the general rule in creating fixed-length records: All fields correspond in length to the field lengths given in the record format.

Remember that character-format digits are not numeric values (see Chapter 1). They are therefore left-justified, the same as any other character-format field. An example of this is the *date* field in Figure 6. If a date contains fewer than four digits, it would be extended on the right by trailing blanks. Realistically, however, few libraries will have to consider manuscripts dated prior to 1000 A.D. Figure 8, a listing of sample book records in the record format described by the logical record layout of Figure 6, shows how fields are left- and right-justified as necessary when creating a fixed-length record file. Remember that each blank takes up a field position and requires storage space as a character in either ASCII or EBCDIC character codes.

Another aspect of interest in Figure 8 is the second record's title field. This field is always 40 characters long, yet the title for the second record originally contained more than 40 bytes. It was

Author	Title	Place of Publication	Publisher	Date	Purchase Price
HAMILTON EDITH	MYTHOLOGY	NEW YORK	MENTOR	194200075	
DAVIS CHARLES H	ILLUSTRATIVE COMPUTER PROGRAMMING FOR LIWESTPORT	GREENWOOD	197400695		
SHEEHY GAIL	PASSAGES	NEW YORK	DUTTON	197401400	
LANCASTER F WILFRID	VOCABULARY CONTROL FOR INFORMATION RETRIWASHINGTONIRP PRESS		197201995		
ROBINSON RICHARD H	BUDDHIST RELIGION	BELMONT CADICKENSON	197000250		

FIELDS: Author — Title — Place of Publication — Publisher — Date — Purchase Price

Figure 8 SAMPLE BOOK RECORDS, USING THE RECORD FORMAT OF FIGURE 6.

therefore *truncated* in order to fit into the 40-byte field provided for the title. In a fixed-length record, with fixed-length fields, truncation means that any data longer than the specified field length will be ignored or lost. When a title has more than 40 characters, the first 40 characters of data are retained and the rest are lost. For a numeric field, however, truncation (like padding) occurs on the left-hand side of the field. Thus, in a *purchase price* field of more than five digits, the leftmost or most significant digits will be lost. Using the record format of Figure 6, a purchase price field of more than $999.99 (internally stored as 99999) will lose the leftmost digit(s). A price of $1,200.00 would be stored as 20000, or an equivalent value of $200.00.

A fixed-length record with internal fields of fixed length clearly has some drawbacks. A glance at Figure 8 shows that many of the title fields have numerous blanks to make them 40 characters long; therefore, space has been wasted. On the other hand, data was lost in the title field of the second record. Depending on the intended use of the data, this may or may not concern the user. A patron receiving a ''New Books Newsletter''might not care if the second item listed has an incomplete title. Or, perhaps, the patron is interested in that title, in which case he is likely to be irked by the ''computer error'' that printed only the first 40 characters of the title. Similarly, truncation might cause serious problems when an attempt is made to store the six-digit purchase price of $1,200.00 in this record format. Vendors will not appreciate receiving a payment of $200.00 instead of $1,200.00. In some cases, truncation might not be important; in others, it may be a serious matter. Therefore, it is necessary to be aware of this phenomenon and to always consider it in designing fixed-length record layouts.

Fixed-length records involve a fundamental problem. By making fixed-length fields longer, few fields in the file's records will contain truncated data. In addition, space wasted on storing blanks and zeros for extended fields will be increased proportionally to the difference between the actual length of data for such individual record fields and the required field length of the layout. In other words, truncation can be eliminated only by declaring that the initial size of a given field will be equivalent to the longest occurrence of that field in the entire file. By declaring the maximum field length—to guarantee no data truncation—the amount of space wasted on padding is maximized for those initial data elements of lesser length than this longest field. The trade-off is one of efficiency in the use of storage space versus the seriousness and extent of truncation.

In the majority of cases, truncation represents loss of data and is an unacceptable alternative. How much extra space is used for blanks or padding may be seen as the variance between the maximum record length—that chosen for the record layout length—and the average and minimum lengths of the input data. For example, if a field in a file layout is specified at seven characters, and the minimal amount of input data is one byte, the potential wasted space is 7 − 1, or 6 bytes. This may not be as serious a misuse of space as a title of 100 spaces, where a title may vary from 1 to 100 characters, a potential variance of 99 bytes.

Analyzing wasted storage space is a fairly simple matter if the input fields can be statistically sampled and graphed. Figure 9 shows a sample distribution of bibliographic data lengths. Often, bell curves are encountered in plotting data lengths. In this example, 400 bytes was found to be the maximum length for bibliographic reference data. The average space requirement was only 200 bytes. The average record, therefore, would require 200 bytes of padding if the record format were based on the maximum possible length to avoid truncation. With a statistical sampling of all proposed file data, the amount of space wasted and the corresponding extent of truncation can be estimated for any given logical record length.

Although fixed-length fields and fixed-length records present such problems, the fixed-length format is by far the most popular in business data processing. Business data typically exhibits less length variance than the data encountered in libraries. Also, it always should be remembered that computers generally work best with uniform data. A commonplace expression is that computers enforce standardization. One reflection of this tendency toward standardization is embodied in the fixed-length field and the fixed-length record. Many programming languages, for example, offer programmers scant or nonexistent facilities for handling fields and records that are not fixed in length. Programming logic

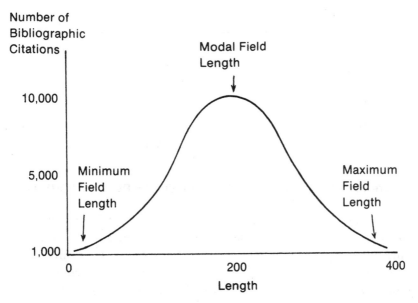

Figure 9   A LENGTH DISTRIBUTION CURVE FOR A STATISTICAL SAMP-
LING OF BIBLIOGRAPHIC CITATIONS.

may be simpler and more clear when working with standardized data elements. The operating system (i.e., software purchased with the computer hardware) may not support record formats other than fixed length. Existing software, programming languages, and programming logic all underlie the general principle of the computer's requirement for data standardization. Fixed-length fields and records are the result of this standardization, so fixed formats have been considered the normal way of handling data and designing logical record layouts.

VARIABLE-LENGTH RECORDS

Variable-length fields and records do exist, however. In a file of variable-length records, the length of each logical record in the file is appropriate to the data or information it contains. If the first record in a file required 128 bytes to contain all its data, the rec-

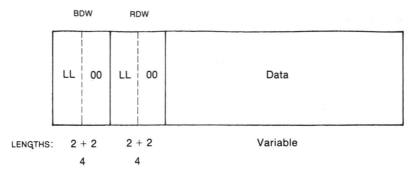

Figure 10   IBM STANDARD VARIABLE-LENGTH RECORD FORMAT.

ord would be (approximately) 128 bytes long. The second and subsequent records in the dataset may be 50 or 200 characters or any other appropriate length (some absolute maximum record size must be declared in many computing systems). Truncation is not a problem, and wasted space through field padding may be either greatly reduced or eliminated.

In manipulating a logical record of variable length, a program must have some method of determining the length of the record. There are two basic approaches to solving this problem: the IBM standard format and the delimiter format. These methods are diagrammed in Figures 10 and 11, respectively.

In the IBM standard variable-length record format, the first eight bytes of the record are reserved for internal use. The first two bytes give the length of the entire record; they are immedi-

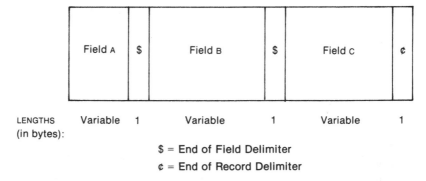

Figure 11   DELIMITER FORMAT FOR VARIABLE-LENGTH RECORDS.

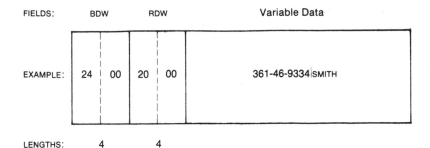

Figure 12   A TYPICAL IBM STANDARD VARIABLE-LENGTH
RECORD FORMAT.

ately followed by two bytes of zeros. Together, these first four
bytes of the record are referred to as the *block descriptor word* (BDW).
All four bytes are in binary, and the length indicated includes the
BDW itself. A four-byte *record descriptor word* (RDW) immediately
follows the BDW. It has the same internal format as the BDW: two
bytes indicating the length of what follows (inclusive) and two
bytes of zeros. Both of these are numeric binary fields. Figure 10
diagrams this record format, and Figure 12 illustrates a typical
variable-length record in this format. From the IBM standard
variable-length record format, it can be observed that a computer
program working with such a record has a simple and standardized way of obtaining the logical length of a given record.[1]

The delimiter method for declaring variable-length records involves specifying a reserved or special character as a *delimiter*. The
delimiters specified may serve to mark the ends of variable-length
fields, and a particular delimiter may be chosen to denote the end
of the variable-length record. A computer program can inspect
each character consecutively for the predefined delimiter, and a
method is provided for determining the lengths and ends of variable-length fields and records.

Figure 11 illustrates the delimiter method for formatting variable-length fields and records. Here a dollar sign $ has been used
to denote the end of a variable field, and the cent sign ¢ marks the
end of the entire variable record.

[1]Detailed information on IBM standards for variable-length records is found in the IBM
manual, *OS/VS2 Data Management Services Guide, GC26-3875-0*, 1st Edition, November
1976, pp. 22–30.

An important point is that the delimiters chosen must never occur within the data fields. A delimiter must be a unique, reserved character, or the end of a field or record will be incorrectly perceived by the computer program as having occurred earlier than was intended. Needless to say, this would cause serious program malfunction and inaccuracies in subsequent processing.

Also, if possible, the delimiter should be a single character. Delimiters of certain character pairs, for example, will render program logic more complex and will involve some processing (CPU) overhead. In some records, however, it will be necessary to use pairs of adjacent characters as delimiters. This might be required either to ensure delimiter uniqueness or to carry information about the following field within the delimiter. In a book record, for example, delimiters might indicate the type of field that follows, such as author, title, imprint, or collation field. *Delimiter typing* might be used as an alternative to having a program know the contents of the fields by their relative positions to other fields in the record.

One occasionally sees variations of the two basic methodologies for creating and handling variable-length records. Figure 13 shows an IBM formatted record, with interior variable-length fields defined by the dollar sign $ delimiter. Figure 14 illustrates another IBM standard variant. Here, two-byte binary field descriptor words (FDWS) indicate the length of the field immediately following; the length indicated includes the two-byte FDW.

Such variants of defining variable-length fields and records usually are peculiar to certain manufacturers or to installations

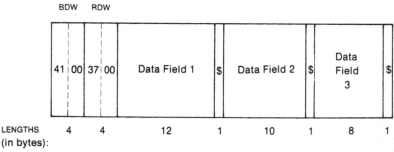

Figure 13 VARIANT-FORMAT VARIABLE-LENGTH RECORD (IBM STANDARD FORMAT, BUT WITH INTERIOR FIELD DELIMITERS).

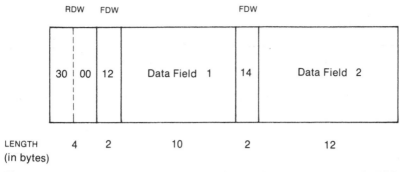

Figure 14 VARIABLE-LENGTH RECORD FORMAT—VARIANT FORMAT.

using them. When they are used, they should be fully described in the accompanying explanation of the program, system, or storage medium in which they are used. The portability of such nonstandard approaches is limited, and data sharing is curtailed.

Most computers and their accompanying software also allow for a user-defined logical record layout: the undefined format. Most systems have rigidly defined layouts for fixed- and variable-length fields and records. The undefined format allows for the use of such variant or nonstandard records.

Finally, there is a way to approximate variable-length records through the use of fixed-length records, which involves designating a particular byte of the fixed-length records as a *continuation character*. This continuation character commonly occurs as the first or the last byte in the fixed-length record. The continuation character indicates that the next fixed-length record is a part of this logical record or that this fixed-length record is the last part of the logical record. Thus, the variable-length logical record will consist of one or more fixed-length portions. The logical record spans a number of fixed-length segments.

Within the logical record, if individual fields are not of fixed length, they may be designated by either delimiters or the fɒw scheme mentioned earlier. Library programmers tend to favor delimiters in such situations. Figure 15 illustrates this alternative with a group of consecutive fixed-length records, each having a continuation character in its first byte. When this character is 1, the next fixed-length record also is considered a part of this logical

Continuation
Characters

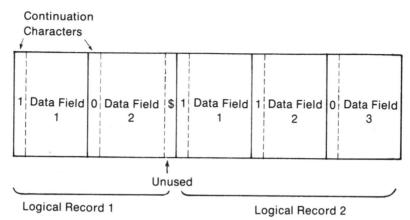

Unused

Logical Record 1   Logical Record 2

Figure 15   APPROXIMATING VARIABLE-LENGTH LOGICAL RECORDS
THROUGH THE USE OF CONSECUTIVE FIXED-LENGTH RECORDS.

record; when the continuation character is 0, the particular fixed-length record under consideration is the last part of the variable-length logical record. When there is some residual or unused space in the last portion of the record, a delimiter might be used to denote this area.

Figure 16 shows the same scheme, using the dollar sign $ delimiter to demarcate the different variable-length fields within each record. The cent sign ¢ delimits residual space at the end of each logical record.

Decreasing the length of the fixed-length records composing the actual logical record has the effect of reducing wasted space. It is more likely that the length of the variable-length record is close to some multiple of the fixed-length record size, so less residual

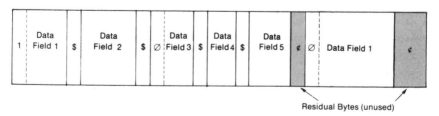

Residual Bytes (unused)

Figure 16   APPROXIMATING VARIABLE-LENGTH LOGICAL RECORDS
THROUGH THE USE OF CONSECUTIVE FIXED-LENGTH RECORDS (IN-CLUDES DELIMITER $ FOR VARIABLE-LENGTH FIELDS).

space results. Obviously, the theoretical limit to this refinement of the approximation process is a fixed-length field of a single byte. But, in reality, since the computer system is aware of only this logical variable-length record as consecutive fixed-length records, there is a practical limit to the length of fixed-length records. This is achieved because the unit of information manipulated in the I/O operation by the program involved is the fixed-length record. I/O operations—the reading or writing of a record—are very expensive in terms of the computer time they use. Achieving a balance would be desirable in this situation; therefore, to accurately approximate a logical variable-length record through the use of contiguous fixed-length records, the fixed-length record must be made short. Otherwise, wasted or residual space will be too large. On the other hand, defining fixed-length records that are too short will result in a large number of I/O operations by any program reading or writing with this file. As I/O operations are expensive in terms of computer time and effort, the program would take too much time on the system. Exactly how much time a typical I/O operation might take will be calculated in Chapter 4.

A general comparison of this methodology to others will be made later in this chapter.

LIBRARY DATA FORMATS

As mentioned previously, in business data processing, most data formats are simple fixed-length records with fixed-length fields. The reasons for this include the logical simplicity inherent in processing fixed-length data, the tendency toward standardization in computer processing, and the usual orientation of programming languages and operating systems toward manipulation of fixed-length data. Most important is the fact that business data processing typically involves a preponderance of relatively short fields in most records. Thus, business data is well suited to fixed-length record formats, because the potential length variance of the data elements is minimal.

The nature of the data stored and processed in libraries is fundamentally different from that of business data. Library data is character-format data. This results in greater potential length variance than in the business environment.

For example, the length variance in library catalog card records is substantial. Most bibliographic items in the catalog require one card, and some require two. But, in the case of serials, government reports, translations, and so on, many cards may be necessary. Consider creating an on-line catalog card retrieval system storing hundreds of thousands of such records. Clearly, fixed-length records imply too much wasted storage space to be practical. Regardless of the processing complexities they may require, variable-length records are mandatory in this situation.

Thus, libraries are essentially concerned with the storage and retrieval of textual information. This sort of *information processing* is fundamentally different from the *data processing* encountered in most businesses. Data processing connotes short fields, many of which are numeric or computational. So, where business can often comfortably choose fixed-length records with a tolerable limit on storage space inefficiencies, libraries frequently are forced to use variable-length or undefined format records.

CONSIDERATIONS

At this point, the use of the aforementioned record formats will be contrasted. When is it appropriate to use fixed-length, variable-length, undefined, or variant record formats?

Fixed-length records with fixed-length fields are certainly the most convenient and should be used whenever possible. When libraries are involved in "information processing," as opposed to traditional "data processing," however, the storage space/truncation dilemma may present a strong argument for the use of either a variable-length or undefined record format. Although the fixed-length record format is standard to almost any computer or manufacturer, the latter two record formats are somewhat machine-dependent in their definition. Whether one uses the IBM standard variable-length format may be dictated by either the computing system or the library's decision, depending on whether the system can support this format. In most computing systems, some degree of formatting flexibility is provided by the undefined record format.

In comparing the two variable-length methods, the IBM version requires that programs be written to update the BDW and RDW length-indicator fields, as necessary. When the record is created, and whenever its length is subsequently altered, the BDW and RDW must be set appropriately.[2]

The delimiter method similarly requires proper placement and updating of the delimiter character as necessary. In addition, each program that manipulates the record must scan for the delimiter. This character-by-character inspection of bytes until the delimiter is found can be fairly time-consuming. Programs using this technique will incur significant processor overhead during their execution.

The method for approximating a variable-length logical record through the use of consecutive fixed-length records involves maintenance of the continuation character and, possibly, of a residual-space delimiter. This approach is obviously quite useful in systems where variable-length format itself is not supported. Since every fixed-length record requires an I/O operation, however, a larger number of I/O operations may be needed in this case. The following section on the "blocking" of records will demonstrate how this problem can be mollified.

BLOCKING OF RECORDS

The blocking of logical records will be explained specifically in terms of tape storage, because it is most easily illustrated by this medium. Remember, however, that blocking is also encountered as a possible storage method on most disks and drums.

The manner in which fixed-length records normally occur on tape storage is shown in Figure 17. Here, each logical fixed-length

---

[2]Programs called *access methods* will sometimes relieve the programmer of responsibility for updating the BDW. Access methods are discussed later in this chapter.

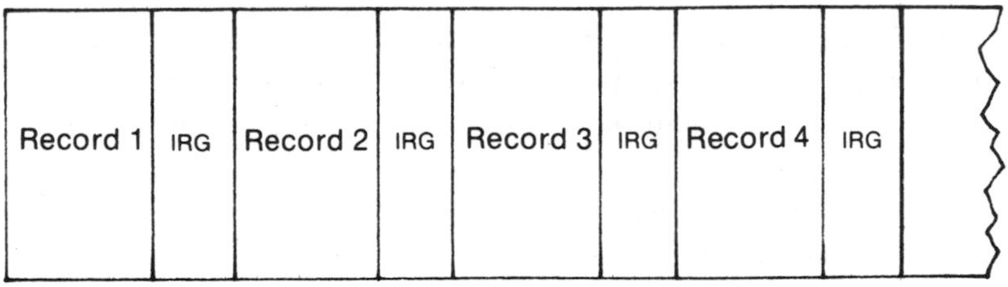

Figure 17   FIXED-LENGTH RECORDS (UNBLOCKED) ON TAPE.

record on the storage medium is separated from the next by an *inter-record gap* (IRG). On most tapes, the IRG is approximately 0.6 inches in length. Its purpose is to allow the tape drive some space to start and stop the fast-moving tape spool between the reading or writing of records. The IRG itself is "wasted" space, where data cannot be stored. Since most tapes have either 800, 1,600, or 6,250 bytes of information stored per inch of tape, it is apparent that the frequent occurrence of this IRG leads to substantial loss of potential storage space.

Blocking of records, illustrated in Figure 18, represents a solution to the excessive storage space devoted to IRGS. Here, three logical records are consecutive; then the IRG occurs. Note that when blocking exists, the IRG is referred to as the *interblock gap* (IBG). The *blocking factor* here is 3, as three logical records are combined into one *physical record*. The number of bytes in the physical record is called the *blocksize*. For fixed-length blocked records, the blocksize will be some multiple of logical record length. The physical record is that unit of information that is read or written in one I/O operation by the tape drive. In other words, one I/O op-

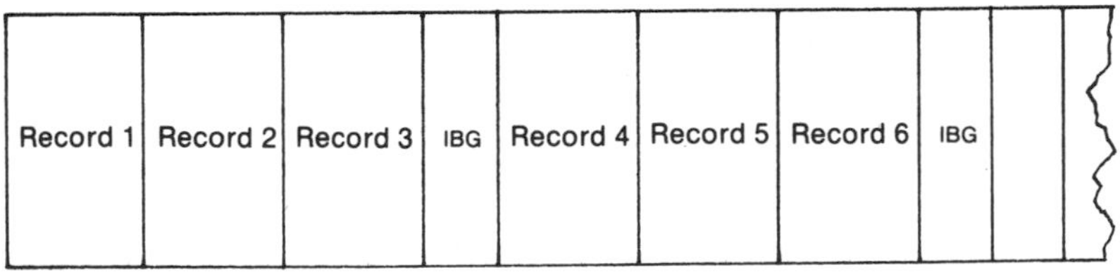

Figure 18   FIXED-LENGTH RECORDS (BLOCKED).

eration will either read or write three logical records at one time. As already mentioned, I/O operations require time on a computer. Exactly how much time they require and the implications of the blocking in this regard will be explored further in Chapter 4.

For now, it is apparent that the more logical records that are blocked together into one physical record, the fewer interblock gaps there will be in the entire file, and the more effective the use of the storage medium will be. In effect, the greater the blocking factor, the more efficient the use of storage space. Some factors in favor of blocking records with the greatest possible blocking factor are:

1. More efficient use of the storage medium. As the ratio of IBGs to logical records on the file drops, proportionately less of the storage medium is expended on IBGs.

2. Less processing time spent on time-consuming I/O operations. Each read or write through the I/O device handles one physical record, not a logical one (unless the system has the unblocked records of Figure 17, in which case a physical record equals a logical record). The number of I/O operations required to read a file drops proportionally to the blocking factor. As the blocking factor is increased, I/O processing time drops.

Factors limiting blocking include the following:

1. Reliability and accuracy are compromised after a certain point, since physical records are the units for I/O operations. Blocks on tapes may range from 80 to 8,000 bytes per physical record. Beyond approximately 10,000 bytes/block, reliability decreases and read/write errors may occur.

2. The computer programs interacting with the file must now extract the desired logical record from the physical block it has read in. The inverse situation—the process of blocking logical records into physical records—must be done before writing records onto the storage medium. Remember that programs prefer to work on the logical unit of information—the logical record. When the physical record does not equal the logical record, a program must refine the former into the latter. Such work is not necessary

where records are already on the storage medium in unblocked form.

Operating system software purchased with the computer usually includes programs called *access methods* to perform the *blocking* and *deblocking* of records prior to actual I/O operations. The availability of access methods for this purpose is an important topic and will be discussed in Chapters 5 and 7 on computing system software. At this time, it should be mentioned that mainframes normally have software convenient for this purpose, minicomputers may or may not have such access methods, and microcomputers currently do not offer them.

3. After a block of data is read in by a program, it must be kept in core storage. One would not want to devote excessive core to space for reading and writing records only. The access methods described normally use a technique called *double buffering*, which means they allocate two such core storage locations or *buffers* for each file to be read or written.

Consider the following example of the space in core used by blocking. A program uses three files, two of which are tape files and one of which is on disk. With 80-byte, fixed-length, unblocked records, total size of the buffers for this program is:[3]

```
2 tape files * 2 buffers/block * 80 bytes/block = 320 bytes
1 disk file  * 2 buffers/block * 80 bytes/block = 160 bytes
                                                   480 bytes
```

Therefore, 480 bytes of core memory are expended for the input/output buffer space needed for this program's input/output buffer operations. But if the blocking factor were 100, there would be:

```
2 tape files * 2 buffers/block * 8,000 bytes/block = 32,000 bytes
1 disk file  * 2 buffers/block * 8,000 bytes/block = 16,000 bytes
                                                      48,000 bytes
```

[3] In equations dealing with computer applications, an asterisk is used to indicate that multiplication should be performed.

Since one *kilobyte, kbyte*, or *K* is equal to 1,024 bytes, this means that a single program will require approximately 48K of core memory for just its I/O operations. In addition, the core memory required for the access-method program itself must be included, since programs occupy core memory while they are being used.

This memory use can significantly limit the potential blocking size in certain situations. Mainframes, for example, typically run a number of programs concurrently, and mini- and microcomputers generally have very limited core. These concepts will be treated in detail in Chapter 5 on multiprogramming and Chapter 11 on microcomputers. Here, the point is that most access methods do use double-buffering techniques and that the program with a large blocking factor and many files will consume considerably more memory space for its I/O operations.

To make these considerations more concrete, calculations concerning blocking factors and their effects on storage medium utilization will be demonstrated in Chapter 4.

VARIABLE-LENGTH BLOCKED RECORDS

Variable-length records also have unblocked and blocked formats. Here again, blocking is used for better storage medium utilization and for minimizing the number of potential I/O operations needed for reading and writing records. Figure 19 shows a tape with variable-length unblocked records, and Figure 20 depicts the blocking of records. Both figures use the IBM standard format for variable-length records.

BDW	RDW	Record 1	IBG	BDW	RDW	Record 2	

Figure 19 VARIABLE-LENGTH RECORDS (UNBLOCKED).

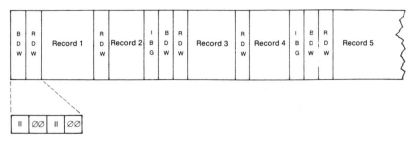

Figure 20   VARIABLE-LENGTH RECORDS (BLOCKED).

Figure 20 shows the reason for the block descriptor word. This four-byte binary field contains the two-byte length of the block followed by two bytes of zeros. The BDW gives a program the length of the variable block in the same manner as the RDW provides the length of a given logical record. BDWs and RDWs, thus, are analogous length descriptors: The first gives the block length; the second gives individual logical record lengths. Both descriptors have the same internal format.

For the sake of completeness, IBM's undefined record format and its normal blocking are shown in Figure 21.

In conclusion, it is advantageous for libraries to choose the standard variable-length formats for their computer systems where variable-length records must be used. Undefined formats are strictly local record layouts that will reduce considerably the value of the data outside the single computing system for which they are created.

Record 1	IBG	Record 2	IBG	Record 3	IBG

Figure 21   IBM UNDEFINED FORMAT RECORDS.

CHAPTER 4

System Storage Mediums

This chapter explores specific storage mediums in order to determine which is most suitable for a certain situation and what combinations of storage devices are appropriate for a computing system.

In addition to considering the nature of storage devices, calculations are presented for estimating parameters such as file size and required storage space and for increasing the effectiveness of storage space utilization. Specific computations are given to substantiate the previously described relationships between blocking factors; other calculations illustrate some relationships in access times of I/O operations. None of these computations requires any mathematical background beyond fundamental algebra.

TAPES

Tape is a common form of computer storage, and the tape drive is its associated I/O device. The tapes consist of a strong, flexible, plastic compound strip to which a ferromagnetic coating adheres. Encoding of data occurs by magnetizing bit signals in the coating.

Individual tapes are surprisingly inexpensive; prices vary from $10 to $25 per tape. For this price, they offer a massive storage medium. Spool lengths range from a few feet to a few thousand feet, and their lengths are a factor in figuring how many bytes of data an individual tape will hold. Another factor is the *recording density* of the tape. Currently, common recording densities are 800 bytes per inch (BPI), 1,600 BPI, and 6,250 BPI. There is no deterioration in recording quality among the varying recording densities; the densities reflect advances in technology only.

Although tapes are inexpensive, tape drives are not. Fortunately, tapes can be kept on-line or off-line. Typically, an installation maintains a *tape library* of off-line tapes. Any particular tape can then be placed on-line immediately prior to scheduling a program that requires access to the data on that tape.

Another characteristic of tapes is that they are highly portable. It is quite easy to send data encoded on tape through the mails.

Occasionally, tapes may need to be cleaned, since small dust particles may prevent accurate reading or writing of data. Also, tapes need to be rewound every few years if not used, or data will become demagnetized.

Tapes are approximately one-half inch wide, with either seven or nine *tracks*, each track representing the space for encoding a bit of data. Figure 22 shows how bytes are spaced on the tape. The *parity bit* is used only to verify the accuracy of the data read from the tape. Parity bits are generated and checked automatically by the tape drive machinery. Nine-track tapes encode bytes vertically in EBCDIC, with one position for the parity bit. Seven-track tapes often are used for ASCII and BCD character codes.

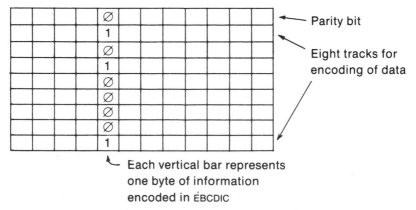

Figure 22 INFORMATION REPRESENTATION ON A NINE-TRACK TAPE.

All tapes have a certain amount of unused slack space—*leaders* and *trailers*—for threading the tape onto the tape drive. *Tape markers* indicate the beginning and end of the tape, and internal *tape marks* denote the beginning and end of the various logical files or datasets. Thus, many different files can be stored on one tape. The tape drive is directed to read and count file marks on the tape until it gets to the dataset to be used. Only one file can be accessed at any given time, however, as tape drives spin the tape past a single *read/write head* for data sensing or writing.

Tapes are protected from accidental writing, with resultant loss of previously existing data, because without a *write-enable ring,* they can be read but not written on by an executing program. The computer operator must write-enable any tape by physically placing a *write-enable ring* on the tape.

Perhaps the single most important characteristic of tape is that it is a *sequential* storage medium only. As shown in Figures 17 through 21, records are stored on tape, one after the other. This means that a computer program can read or write records in sequential order only. If the program is directed to read only the 120th record on the tape, it must read the first 119 records to get to the 120th. There is no quick way to get to the 120th record directly, such as provided by *direct access* devices.

Recall the example of cyclical program processing logic (discussed in Chapter 3), where records are read and processed one after the other until the end of the file is reached. In this situation, where every record in the file would be processed in sequence, tape is a highly suitable storage medium. For example, library patron information might be kept on a sequential tape file and ordered on ascending patron identification number. In order to print a listing of all library cards that are no longer valid, a program would read each record sequentially and check to see if that patron's borrower's card is outdated. If it is, the program would print out the invalid record and go on to process the next record in the file. But if the patron's card is still valid, the program would just ignore it and read the next record in the file. In this manner, sequentially accessed storage mediums can be useful in many situations.

But what if only a particular patron record was requested from the file? On the average, it would be necessary to search half the file before finding that specific record. In a file of any size, this would entail many slow tape I/O operations and considerable time for the program to finish. Tape drives cannot provide *direct access* to a given record based on a certain field's contents. In this example, the field is the patron identification number, which is referred to as the record's *key*. When a user is searching a sequential storage medium for a record having a specific key, there is no recourse to reading each consecutive record until one with the desired key is found. Tape, therefore, is not suitable for the direct processing of records.

As an example of a situation where a sequentially processed storage medium like tape is not appropriate, on-line circulation control systems should be considered. With these systems, either a librarian or a patron enters transaction data concerning the borrower and the borrowed item(s). If, for some reason, the transaction is not valid, the computer system quickly provides an appropriate response. A computing system that responds within reasonable waiting time is said to be a *real-time* system. Tapes do not operate rapidly enough for this quick response, since they cannot directly access whatever records might be involved. In this case, an efficient system would require direct access on such keys as the patron or bibliographic identification numbers.

Tapes are labelled in two ways. *Internal labels* are written directly on the beginning of the tapes, in the manner of the file(s) stored on them. These labels identify the tape and its contents to programs using the tape. *External labels* are handwritten, gummed labels affixed to the sides of the tape reels for easy user identification. External labels usually contain a unique identification number, a description of file contents, names, dates, and, possibly, obsolescence dates. It is important that these labels contain all the information to be remembered concerning tape contents. In the library with only a few tapes, the tape label data will soon be forgotten if it is not written on the label. In a library with a large number of computer tapes, the unmarked or improperly marked tape may be lost permanently.

TAPE CALCULATIONS

Two main methods are used to physically encode data bits on a tape. The *nonreturn to zero, impulsed* (NRZI) method interprets any change in recording flux as a 1 bit. The absence of any change in magnetism on a tape represents a 0 bit. In effect, 1 bits are recorded on the tape; 0 bits are not. In *phase-encoded* (PE) recording, both 0 and 1 bits are recorded on the tape's surface.

Both methods have check bits recorded with each block of data (in addition to the parity bits). These check bits are automatically generated or read by the tape drive to ensure data integrity.

Figures 23 and 24 illustrate the check bits encoded per block of data for NRZI and phase-encoded methods, respectively. NRZI results in only two bytes of check bits per block, so these bytes normally are of little consequence in storage calculations. Phase-

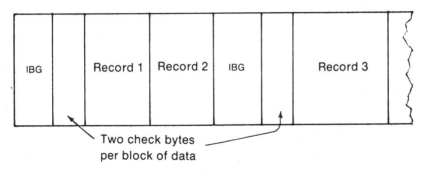

Figure 23 NRZI CHECK BITS PER BLOCK OF DATA.

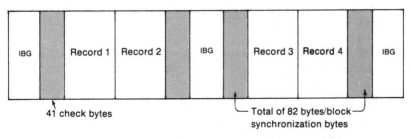

Figure 24 PHASE-ENCODED CHECK BYTES PER BLOCK OF DATA.

encoding results in a total of 82 *synchronization bytes* per block, and they cannot be ignored in accurate storage calculations.

There are three main questions that knowledgeable librarians would like to be able to answer in reference to tape storage space. These questions and sample relevant calculations follow. None requires any advanced knowledge of mathematics other than basic algebra.

Tape Question 1: If tape length and recording density are known, how is the number of logical records that can be stored on that tape determined?

The two basic equations used here are:

$$\frac{\text{Blocksize}}{800 \text{ BPI}} + 0.6 \text{ inches IBG for NRZI tapes at 800 BPI} \qquad (1)$$

$$\frac{\text{Blocksize} + 82 \text{ check bytes}}{1,600 \text{ BPI}}$$
$$+ 0.6 \text{ inches IBG for } 1,600 \text{ BPI phase-encoded tape} \qquad (2)$$

In both cases,

$$\text{Blocksize} = \text{Logical record length} * \text{Blocking factor}$$

Note that, for simplification, only fixed-length logical records will be used.

Example 1. Given a file of 150-byte logical records to be stored on tape, with a blocking factor of 30 logical records per block, how many logical records could be stored on 1,200 feet of 800 BPI NRZI tape?

Number of bytes per block is:

150 bytes/logical record * 30 logical records/block = 4,500 bytes/block

Number of inches needed per block is:

$$\frac{4,500 \text{ bytes/block}}{800 \text{ BPI}} + 0.6 \text{ inches IBG} =$$

6.2 inches required for each block

Number of blocks needed is:

$$\frac{1,200 \text{ feet of tape} * 12 \text{ inches/foot}}{6.2 \text{ inches/block}} =$$

2,322 whole blocks needed (do not round up)

Number of records that could fit on the tape is:

2,322 blocks could fit * 30 logical records/block = 69,660 logical records could fit on the given tape

Example 2. Same problem except for 1,200 feet of 1,600 BPI phase-encoded tape as the storage medium. As always, it should be assumed that only complete blocks will be stored on the tape.

Number of bytes per block is:

150 bytes/logical record * 30 logical records/block = 4,500 bytes/block

Number of inches needed per block is:

$$\frac{4,500 \text{ bytes/block} + 82 \text{ synchronization bytes}}{1,600 \text{ BPI}} + 0.6 \text{ IBG} =$$

3.5 inches required for each block

Number of blocks is:

$$\frac{1,200 \text{ feet of tape} * 12 \text{ inches/foot}}{3.5 \text{ inches/block}} = 4,114 \text{ whole blocks}$$
(do not round up)

Number of records that could fit on the tape is:

4,114 blocks * 30 logical records/block = 123,420 logical records could fit on the given tape

Tape Question 2: How many feet of a given tape are needed to store a given file?

Example 3. Given a sequential file of 14,000 logical records, each 100 bytes long, with a blocking factor of 70 records per block, how many feet of tape would be required to store this file on an 800 BPI NRZI tape?

The number of bytes per block is:

70 logical records/block * 100 bytes/logical record = 7,000 bytes/block

Number of inches of tape per block is:

$$\frac{7,000 \text{ bytes/block}}{800 \text{ BPI}} + 0.6 \text{ inches IBG} = 9.35 \text{ inches required/block}$$

Number of blocks needed therefore is:

$$\frac{14,000 \text{ logical records in file}}{70 \text{ logical records/block}} = 200 \text{ blocks needed to hold file}$$

Number of feet of tape needed to hold the file is:

$$\frac{200 \text{ blocks needed} * 9.35 \text{ inches required/block}}{12 \text{ inches/foot}} =$$

155.8 feet of tape for this file

Example 4. Same problem as Example 3, but determine instead how many feet of 1,600 BPI PE tape would be needed to hold this file.

The number of bytes per block is:

70 logical records/block * 100 bytes in a logical record = 7,000 bytes/block

Number of inches of tape per block is:

$$\frac{7,000 \text{ bytes/block} + 82 \text{ synchronization bytes/block}}{1,600 \text{ BPI}} + 0.6 \text{ inches IBG} =$$

5.03 inches required/block

Number of blocks needed is:

$$\frac{14,000 \text{ logical records in file}}{70 \text{ logical records/block}} = 200 \text{ blocks needed to hold file}$$

Number of feet of tape needed to hold the file is:

$$\frac{200 \text{ blocks needed} * 5.03 \text{ inches required/block}}{12 \text{ inches/foot}} =$$

83.8 feet of 1,600 BPI tape required to hold this file

Tape Question 3: Tape utilization is a measure expressing the efficiency of tape usage as a storage medium. Effective storage use of the tape is given in the form of the percentage of potential storage space on the tape actually used in this capacity. In general terms, effective tape utilization may be calculated by this equation:

$$\text{Percent utilization} = \frac{\left(\dfrac{\text{Blocksize}}{\text{BPI}}\right)}{\left(\dfrac{\text{Blocksize}}{\text{BPI}}\right) + \text{IBG size}} * 100 \text{ percent}$$

For 800 BPI NRZI tapes, this yields the general form of:

$$\text{Percent utilization} = \frac{\left(\dfrac{\text{Blocksize}}{800 \text{ BPI}}\right)}{\left(\dfrac{\text{Blocksize}}{800 \text{ BPI}}\right) + 0.6 \text{ inches/IBG}} * 100 \text{ percent}$$

For 1,600 BPI PE tapes, this equation is:

Percent utilization =

$$\frac{\left(\dfrac{\text{Blocksize}}{1,600 \text{ BPI}}\right)}{\left(\dfrac{\text{Blocksize} + 82 \text{ synchronization bytes}}{1,600 \text{ BPI}}\right) + 0.6 \text{ inches/IBG}} * 100 \text{ percent}$$

In all of these equations,

Blocksize = Logical record size * Number of logical records/physical record

Of course, the number of logical records per physical record is simply another way of referring to the blocking factor.

Example 5. Suppose that 100-byte logical records are to be stored on 1,600 BPI PE tape. Compute the effective tape utilization when the records are stored using a blocking factor of 5.

Percent utilization =

$$\frac{\left(\dfrac{5 \text{ log. recs./block} * 100 \text{ bytes log. rec.}}{1,600 \text{ BPI}}\right)}{\left(\dfrac{5 \text{ log. recs./block} * 100 \text{ bytes/log. rec.} + 82 \text{ sync. bytes}}{1,600 \text{ BPI}}\right)}$$

To this equation, add 0.6 inches/IBG to the denominator, then multiply the entire number by 100 percent. This yields the overall result of 32.4 percent effective tape utilization.

Example 6. Using the same logical records and tape specifications given in Example 5, compute tape utilization as a storage medium for the following blocking factors:

$$1,2,3,4,5,10,15,20,25,50$$

Draw a graph of tape utilization as a percentage (vertical axis) against the blocking factor (horizontal axis).

The computations are performed like those shown in Example 5. Table 2 gives the results of these calculations, and Figure 25 graphs the results.

From the graph of the results, the relationship between tape utilization and blocking factors becomes evident. There is a law of diminishing returns for storage utilization as the blocking factor increases beyond a certain point. But increasing the blocking factor to some small degree beyond 1 (unblocked records) seems to help storage utilization considerably. This graph provides the basis for the advantages and limits mentioned earlier, concerning blocking for effective utilization of a storage medium.

TAPE TIMING

The basic approach demonstrated in the calculations for tape storage and utilization figures for 800 BPI NRZI and 1,600 PE tapes is valid for other tape densities as well. Effective use of storage is something librarians, administrators, and other information scientists need to be generally familiar with.

Next, sample calculations will be presented for the time required to perform tape I/O operations. These equations are specific to the IBM 3420 Model 5 tape drive and, thus, are considered *machine-dependent.* Calculations for other makes and models of tape units may have other equations, but the principles involved are the same as those to be shown. These calculations are included in

TABLE 2 Effective Tape Utilization as a Function of Blocking Factor

Blocking Factor	Effective Tape Utilization %
1	8.8
2	16.1
3	22.4
4	27.7
5	32.4
10	49.0
15	59.0
20	65.7
25	70.6
50	82.8

order to demonstrate exactly how much time I/O operations require, relative to the processing speed of the CPU. Before reading this section, the reader may wish to look at Figure 26, which provides the relationships between various timing units used in reference to computer operations.

Timing Example 1. Given a sequential tape file of 14,000 logical records, each 100 bytes long, with a blocking factor of 70 records per block, on 800 BPI NRZI tape, how long would it take to read this file?

The general equation for milleseconds (ms) to read a block, specific to the model tape drive used here,[1] is:

$$4.8 \text{ ms tape passing time } + \frac{\text{Blocksize}}{100 \text{ ms data transfer rate}}$$

For this problem, the solution is:

$$4.8 \text{ ms tape passing time } + \frac{100 \text{ bytes/logical record } * 70 \text{ records/block}}{100 \text{ ms data transfer rate}} =$$

74.8 ms required to read one block from the tape

The time required to read the file is:

$$\frac{200 \text{ blocks } * 74.8 \text{ ms/block}}{1,000 \text{ ms in a second}} = 14.96 \text{ seconds to read the file}$$

[1] IBM 3420 Model 5 tape drive operating in continuous mode.

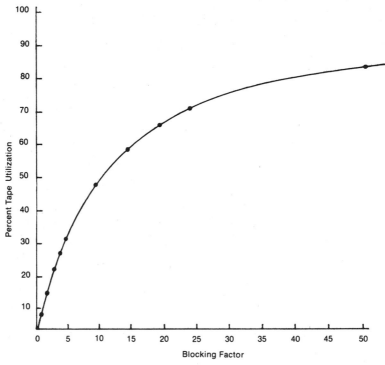

Figure 25   EFFECTIVE TAPE UTILIZATION AS A FUNCTION OF BLOCK-ING FACTOR.

This result, 14.96 seconds, is a very long time in cpu terms, as is 74.8 ms. Relative times can be illustrated by assuming that it takes 2 microseconds (μs) per each instruction executed on an IBM Series 360 computer. The cpu could have executed these instructions in the time it took the tape drive to read in a single block of data:

$$\frac{74.8 \text{ ms/block read } * \text{ 1,000 ms/second}}{2 \text{ } \mu\text{s/instruction executed}} = 37,400 \text{ instructions}$$

Therefore, the computer could have performed 37,400 instructions in the time the tape drive took to read in a single block of data. Clearly, input/output operations, which involve mechanical or physical movement at some point, are not nearly as fast as the electronic calculations of the central processor.

Unit	Abbreviation	Length (in seconds)
Millesecond	ms	1/1,000 Second
Microsecond	μs	1/1,000,000 Second
Nanosecond	ns	1/1,000,000,000 Second

Figure 26   COMPUTER TIMING UNITS.

Timing Example 2. This example is the same as Timing Example 1, except that the file is on 1,600 BPI PE tape.

The general formula for milleseconds to read one block is similar to that for 800 BPI NRZI tape, except that 82 synchronization bytes per block must again be considered:

$$4.8 \text{ ms tape passing time} + \frac{\text{Blocksize} + 82 \text{ synchronization bytes/block}}{200 \text{ ms data transfer rate}}$$

Time required to read one block of data is:

$$\frac{4.8 \text{ ms} + [(70 \text{ records/block} * 100 \text{ bytes/record}) + 82 \text{ synchronization bytes/block}]}{200 \text{ ms data transfer rate}} =$$

40.21 ms to read one block of data

Time for reading the entire file is:

$$\frac{200 \text{ blocks} * 40.21 \text{ ms/block}}{1,000 \text{ ms/second}} = 8.04 \text{ seconds to read the file}$$

Assuming two microseconds per instruction executed by the IBM 360 central processor:

$$\frac{40.21 \text{ ms/block read}}{2 \text{ μs/instruction executed}} * 1,000 \text{ ms/second} = 20,105 \text{ instructions}$$

Therefore, 20,105 instructions could be executed by the CPU in the time it takes to read one block of data off the tape.

The disparity between the rate at which the CPU can execute instructions and the rate at which I/O operations can be performed is basic to the concept of *multiprogramming*. Instead of allowing the CPU to sit idle whenever a program performs an I/O (read/write) operation, the CPU could be performing a lot of work while the tape drive is performing its task. By placing the program that is waiting for I/O into a "holding pattern" and saving its current status somewhere in core, another program can be started on the CPU. When this new program is finished (or when it too becomes *blocked* for I/O), the original program can be brought back to finish processing. This method of switching between programs, while some wait for I/O, is *multiprogramming,* or *concurrent execution*. The process of putting a program on "hold" while its I/O is being performed is called putting it into the *wait state*. Small *peripheral processors* or *channels* are responsible for actually directing the I/O operation while the program is in the wait state, and the CPU begins executing another program. Channels are processors similar to the CPU, except that they are much less powerful. They are able to perform only the simple and limited instructions needed to direct I/O. Thus, it is economically worthwhile to have channels perform these tasks while the CPU does actual program execution. Most mainframes have a number of channels in the system, in addition to the CPU.

Multiprogramming and the extent of its use in computing systems are vitally relevant to the value of any computing system. These topics should not be the esoteric preserve of the programming professionals. As computer users, librarians and administrators need to understand these concepts and comprehend how computers operate before they are able to judge computer systems. These topics will be discussed at length in Chapter 5, on operating systems software.

DISKS

Disk drives are a common I/O device and are associated with the storage medium of the *disk pack*. As illustrated in Figure 27, a disk

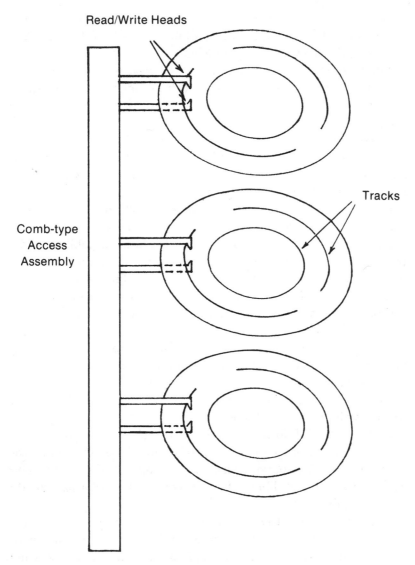

Read/Write Heads

Comb-type
Access
Assembly

Tracks

Figure 27   THE MAJOR COMPONENTS OF A DISK DRIVE.

drive consists of a number of flat recording surfaces, each somewhat like a phonograph disk. Data recording occurs in the ferromagnetic coating on these surfaces; both sides of each "platter"
are used for recording. The number of platters actually in a disk

pack is dependent on the particular brand of drive. IBM 2314 disk packs have 20 recording surfaces, while the IBM 3340 has 12. Data recording densities also vary widely.

Figure 27 shows the circumference, or *track*, on a recording surface. Tracks on each surface are concentric rings that do not spiral inward as in a phonograph record. Every track on the disk has the same maximum data storage capacity.

A comb-type access assembly is attached to the read/write heads, which allows for access to data. A single head is provided for each recording surface. The combination of tracks under the read/write heads at any one time is a *cylinder*.

On most disk drives, the *disk pack*—or collection of recording surfaces—is detachable from the access mechanism and the disk cabinet. These removable packs offer physical portability of the packs and their data. *Fixed-head* drives do not allow pack portability, but do provide slightly faster access time for any data on the disk. The portable-pack type of disk drive is the most common. For packs that are portable, external labelling is recommended to avoid confusing one pack with another.

Since disks spin constantly while the computer is running, there is the possibility of data loss under conditions such as a power failure. But equipment from most manufacturers is sophisticated enough that this possibility is infrequent to highly remote. Most installations keep duplicate or *backup copies* of any important data stored on disk for this reason. Since tapes are such an inexpensive off-line storage medium, it is not uncommon to run a program to back up important disk data on tape. The tape can then be stored in the tape library for subsequent data *reloading,* should this be required.

Libraries, particularly, should be aware of proper backup procedures. Where information storage and retrieval are concerned, it makes little sense to lose information. Library data processing should follow thoroughly modern and complete backup procedures, since the capture of bibliographic and other data in machine-readable forms is a time-consuming and expensive task.

Disks are fundamentally different from tape in that disks allow both sequential and direct access to the records stored on-line. A program can sequentially access records by reading one after another. But it can also directly access a record with a given key through the use of an access-method program. If a file of bibliographic records is stored on main entry, an item by James Joyce is accessible directly—through a single "read" instruction in a program. Recall that with the sequential medium of tape, this program would be forced to read all previous records until the desired record was reached. The potential of disks to act as either a sequential or a direct access device makes them especially valuable i/o devices.

In general, disks offer fairly massive storage. They are somewhat expensive per drive, but the expense per byte stored is reasonable. Like tape, cost per byte stored on-line is much higher than if stored off-line. Storing data on-line takes up the resource of a disk drive as well as the less expensive pack itself. Off-line storage requires the disk pack only, once the data has been encoded on that pack.

Disks have the same record formats and blocking factor considerations as tapes. The comments on these topics in Chapter 3 apply generally to disks as well. Storage utilization and access time are considerations in disk file design, similar to those for tape. At this point, some space computations will be worked through to show how to choose appropriate blocking factors for disk files.

Disk Problem 1: Assume a program is to process a sequential file stored on an IBM 3330 disk pack. The logical record length is 75 bytes, and the file contains 20,000 records.

> *Part A.* What blocking factor should be used for the minimum number of cylinders that will contain the file? How many cylinders are used?

If one reads an IBM manual summarizing 3330 disk characteristics, it is apparent that maximum block capacity for one block per track is 13,030 bytes. To calculate the blocking factor, the computation is:

> 13,030 bytes/block * 1 record/75 bytes = 173 records/block (blocking factor of 173)

To estimate cylinders needed for this file:

$$20{,}000 \text{ records} * \frac{1 \text{ track}}{173 \text{ records}} * \frac{1 \text{ cylinder}}{19 \text{ tracks}} =$$

6.1 or 7 cylinders needed to hold this file

The figure of 19 tracks per cylinder available for programmer use for the 3330 disk also is taken from the IBM manual. Many computer companies print this type of specific device information on *reference summary cards,* which are convenient tables for quick information and device statistics. The IBM 3330 Disk Reference Summary Card is reproduced in Appendix B.

> *Part B.* What blocking factor would be required for two blocks of data per track? How many cylinders would be needed in this case?

From the 3330 reference summary tables, two blocks per track allow a maximum of 6,447 bytes in each block. The calculation is:

$$\frac{6{,}447 \text{ bytes}}{\text{block}} * \frac{1 \text{ logical record}}{75 \text{ bytes}} = 85 \text{ logical records per block}$$

The blocking factor is 85. To compute the number of cylinders required:

$$20{,}000 \text{ records} * \frac{1 \text{ block}}{85 \text{ records}} * \frac{1 \text{ track}}{2 \text{ blocks}} * \frac{1 \text{ cylinder}}{19 \text{ tracks}} =$$

6.2 or 7 cylinders are needed for the file

> *Part C.* How much space would be required if this same file were unblocked?

The manual shows that 62 logical records are available per track with unblocked records 75 bytes in length. Thus,

$$20{,}000 \text{ records} * \frac{1 \text{ track}}{62 \text{ records}} * \frac{1 \text{ cylinder}}{19 \text{ tracks}} =$$

16.9 or 17 whole cylinders are required

Timing calculations for disks involve three quantities: *seek time,* which is the time it takes for a read/write head to get to the proper track; *rotational delay,* which is the length of time a read/write head must wait until the desired record is beneath it (remember that the disk surfaces are always rotating); and *data transfer rate,* which is the speed at which the data is actually transferred from the device. Figure 28 gives these data for the IBM 3330 disk pack. It also lists the abbreviations to be used in the following problems.

Part D. Given the same information as in the previous problem, how long (on the average) would it take to read the file when blocked as in Part B? Assume that the reader is the only user of the disk pack.

Time to read a block is:

$$8.4 \text{ ms average RD } + \frac{1.24 \text{ } \mu\text{s DTR}}{\text{byte}} * \frac{75 \text{ bytes}}{\text{record}} * \frac{85 \text{ records}}{\text{block}} =$$

$8.4 + 7.9 = 16.3$ ms to read one block

Time required to read a track is:

$$\frac{2 \text{ blocks}}{\text{track}} * \frac{16.3 \text{ ms}}{\text{block}} = \frac{32.6 \text{ ms}}{\text{track}} = 32.6 \text{ ms to read a track}$$

Time to read a cylinder is:

$$10 \text{ ms seek time } + \frac{19 \text{ tracks}}{\text{cylinder}} * \frac{32.6 \text{ ms}}{\text{track}} = \frac{629.4 \text{ ms}}{\text{cylinder}} \text{ are required to read the cylinder}$$

(use minimum seek time since there is a single user of the pack)

Approximate time to read the whole file is:

$$7 \text{ cylinders } * \frac{629.4 \text{ ms}}{\text{cylinder}} = 4,405.8 \text{ ms or about } 4.4 \text{ seconds}$$

or, more accurately:

$$6.2 \text{ cylinders } * \frac{629.4 \text{ ms}}{\text{cylinder}} = 3,902.3 \text{ ms or about } 3.9 \text{ seconds}$$

Part E. How long (on the average) would it take to read the file when blocked, as in Part B, if other users were accessing the same disk pack?

Seek Time (ST)

Minimum	10 ms
Average	30 ms
Maximum	55 ms

Rotational Delay (RD)

Minimum	0 ms
Average	8.4 ms
Maximum	16.7 ms

Data Transfer Rate (DTR)

1.24 μs/byte

(806 kbytes/second)

Figure 28   IBM 3330 DISK DEVICE TIMING CHARACTERISTICS (SEE APPENDIX B FOR MORE COMPLETE 3330 DISK CHARACTERISTICS).

Time to read a block is:

30 ms + 8.4 ms average RD + 7.9 ms =
(take average   (time for total
seek time since other   data transfer rate
users are accessing   computed in
same disk pack)   Part D)

46.3 ms to read one block

Approximate time to read the entire file is:

$$7 \text{ cylinders} * \frac{19 \text{ tracks}}{\text{cylinder}} * \frac{2 \text{ blocks}}{\text{track}} * \frac{46.3 \text{ ms}}{\text{block}} =$$

12,315.8 ms or 12.3 seconds

or, more closely:

$$6.2 \text{ cylinders} * \frac{19 \text{ tracks}}{\text{cylinder}} * \frac{2 \text{ blocks}}{\text{track}} * \frac{46.3 \text{ ms}}{\text{block}} =$$

10,908.3 ms or 10.9 seconds

Part F. In this final disk computation, direct access to records is desired, with a data length of 1,496 bytes and a key length of 14. Assuming no blocking, how many records can be put on each track of the 3330 disk pack?

The length of the record here is the length of the data plus the key length or:

1,496 bytes/logical record + 14 bytes key length = 1,510 bytes total

Looking either in the manual or on a reference summary card for the 3330 disk, the user finds that seven blocks of this size are available on one track. Since the blocking factor is 1 (unblocked records), this also means seven records fit on one track.
The time required to read one block is:

$$30 \text{ ms average seek time} + 8.4 \text{ ms average RD} + \frac{1,496 \text{ bytes}}{\text{block}} *$$

$$\frac{1.24 \ \mu s}{\text{byte}} \text{ DTR} = 30 \text{ ms} + 8.4 \text{ ms} + 1.9 \text{ ms} =$$

40.3 ms to read one block

For the particular tape and disk timing examples given, it is apparent that I/O operations for tape and disk take roughly the same amount of time.

DRUMS

A drum is another form of storage device allowing for either sequential or direct access to records. Devices that permit either form of access to stored data are called *direct access storage devices* or DASDS.

Drums are cylindrical objects with data encoded in tracks around their surfaces. Figure 29 shows how each track has its own read/write head. There is no seek time, such as disks have, for

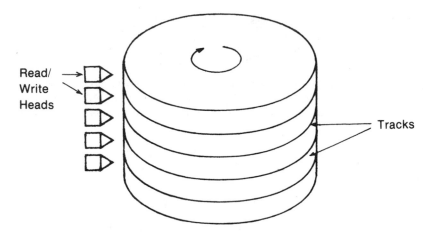

Figure 29   A DIRECT ACCESS DRUM HAS ONE READ/WRITE HEAD FOR EACH TRACK.

read/write heads to find the proper track for a given record. Therefore, drums are faster I/O devices than are disks in terms of direct data access times. Drums, however, do not allow for detaching the cylinder from the rest of the mechanism and are not considered portable. Any data on a drum is on-line at all times. Furthermore, drums hold less information and cost more per byte of data stored than disks. These factors are reflected in the relative position of drum storage in the memory hierarchy chart of Figure 5.

Due to higher storage costs, drums are not used as frequently as disks. Drums are most suited to applications where the need for faster access time can be shown to justify higher costs. Library real-time systems discussed earlier would be occasions for using drums to perform library tasks. Real-time systems for serials check-in, circulation control, cataloging bibliographic items, and information retrieval systems all might fit into this category.

MASS STORAGE SYSTEM

A mass storage system (MSS) allows for massive on-line data storage: Its exact nature depends on manufacturers. Data cells, which are cylinders with magnetically encoded strips on their sides, may be considered in this family of devices. They provide for (relatively) slow direct and sequential record access. Other systems use high-density disks in special configurations or high-density tapes.

At this time, MSSS are expensive and are used primarily at very large installations. Future information storage and retrieval systems, as envisioned for libraries by experts such as F. Wilfrid Lancaster,[2] probably will be based on improved forms of MSSS.

OTHER STORAGE MEDIUMS

Most other I/O devices are considered primarily as data-entry or display devices. Teletypes and CRTs have little or no data storage capacity. Printers function as output devices, and data can be stored in their printouts. It is inconvenient, however, to keep any more than the most frequently referenced data stored on computer paper. In addition, the listing itself is not machine readable.

Punched paper tape, in five-channel and eight-channel versions, was a common method of storage in early computing systems. Paper tape cannot be wound through the reader/puncher very fast without breaking, however, and it presently is used almost exclusively in older computing systems.

Although data may be stored in machine-readable form on computer cards, cards are used primarily as a data-entry medium. On a per-byte basis, cards are a bulky form of data storage. Furthermore, humidity and other environmental factors can warp or destroy computer cards. Most installations using cards do so only for initial data entry into the computing system. After input is completed, the cards are discarded, while the data resides permanently in tape or disk storage.

As mentioned in Chapter 1, there are numerous I/O devices, some having storage capacity. Those having particular relevance to mini- and microcomputer systems will be discussed in Chapter 11. Others, such as optical character readers (OCRs), card punches, and various devices, are not seen often in libraries.

[2]F. Wilfrid Lancaster. "Vocabulary Control in Information Retrieval Systems." In: *Advances in Librarianship.* Volume 7. Edited by Melvin J. Voight and Michael H. Harris. New York, Academic Press, 1977.

CHAPTER 5

Operating Systems Software

The term "software" refers to computer programs. Software allows the computer to do useful work. Whatever program is executing on the central processor at any time is the director for any work the computer is able to perform.

Programs consist of individual computer instructions that are executed in a step-sequential manner. Decisions can be embodied in programs by simple logical testing for a given situation. Depending on the results of such testing, a *branch* instruction may be performed that points to the next instruction to be executed—an instruction other than the next one occurring in the program. In this way, a *transfer of control* occurs within the program. Conditional statements and transfers of control are the means by which a computer program is given its "decision-making" abilities.

Since the programs determine the nature, quality, and type of work being done at any time, software is a critical part of the system. It is as crucial as the computer system's hardware components. In recent computer research and development, many experts would venture to state that software is more important than hardware. A comparison between the two hardly seems necessary—both are essential. What is important is that the significance of software appropriate to the tasks to be performed must be fully appreciated. In the case of library information processing, those persons responsible for administering and directing the computing system need to be especially aware of software requirements and concepts.

Software can be divided into two broad groups. The first category consists of programs purchased by the installation or library. These are generalized or *canned* programs, sold by vendors as a profit-making venture because there are sufficient numbers of computer users desiring to run programs for similar purposes.

Programs produced on-site—by library programmer/analysts—compose the second group. These programs are produced to perform specific, localized functions.

Purchased programs can be further subdivided into two smaller categories: operating systems software and systems support software. The *operating system* is the control program for a computing system. This large program is purchased (or rented or otherwise obtained) and provided by the manufacturer when the computer is obtained. The control program is responsible for aspects of systems control such as selecting, scheduling, and setting up programs to run; communicating with the operator through the systems console; and, generally, managing the finite resources of a computer system during its operation.

Systems support software consists of programs available to aid user programs; they are distinct from the operating system program. Systems support programs include utility programs, language translators, text editors, and other programs. In Chapters 7 and 8, this software will be defined and analyzed in terms of information retrieval needs. In this chapter, operating systems software will be discussed.

OPERATING SYSTEMS

The *operating system, monitor, executor,* or *control program* is a computer program basic to the computing system for directing the overall operation of the computer.

The operating system has two primary purposes. First, it functions to aid its users, such as library programmers, in running programs on the computing system more easily. Without the aid of the operating system, most applications programmers would not be able to run programs on the system. Computers have innumerable low-level details that must be attended to in order to perform the most elementary tasks. For example, even the simplest computer program reads data from a computer card. Recall the earlier discussion on the channels that tell the I/O device to read the card. Routinely, the operating system handles the very detailed and complex programming necessary to arrange for proper reading of the data card by the channel. The control program shields the local applications programmer from having to work out the minute, hardware-dependent aspects of channels and other system realities. The local applications programmer writes a program to direct the CPU within the rules of a programming language, in order to establish reliable and sufficient system operation.

The second function of the operating system is to enhance the efficiency of the computing system as a whole. A computer system may be viewed as a system for performing work with finite resources. It may have, for example, one tape drive and eight disk drives. A well-written control program knows how and when to allocate these resources in order to achieve maximum system efficiency. If some control programs are better than others in their performance of these tasks, then what is a ''good'' operating system? More important, what is a ''good'' operating system for a library?

THE PROCESS VIEW

One way to consider an operating system and its functions is by following the progress of a program, or *job*, submitted to the system. Figure 30 shows a job that will be submitted to the computing system through the card reader.

The first few cards to go through the reader are *job control language* (JCL). Since the operating system is allocating limited system resources, JCL makes a declaration of the resources the job will need; that is, JCL communicates with the control program to relay specific job characteristics.

The computer program follows the JCL and is written in a par-

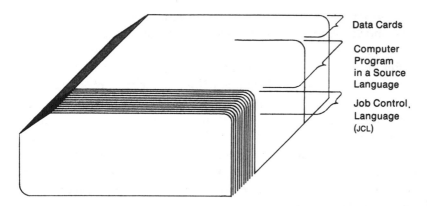

Figure 30 A PROGRAM OR *JOB* BEING SUBMITTED TO THE COMPUT-ING SYSTEM.

ticular computer or *programming language,* referred to as the *source language.* Data needed for input to the program may follow the program itself. Note that if data were needed from a tape or disk file, the jcl would have communicated this requirement to the operating system.

While the program is being read into the system through the card reader, the operating system takes over, directing various steps in the program's life until it leaves the system. The operating system program consists of a number of subprograms that will interact with or act upon the job at various points in its life cycle. The *spooler* program will copy cards read into the system onto a temporary storage device, such as disk storage. Meanwhile, the jcl *scanner* or jcl *monitor* program will read the job's jcl to determine what resources the job requests. Should there be a jcl error, in many systems the jcl scanner program has the authority to delete the job. It prints out the job immediately, with jcl errors indicated by standard error messages. Many computer systems *multiprogram,* that is, allow more than one program to be ready for execution at any given time. Thus, the processor can switch between programs as certain ones request time-consuming i/o operations. The programs requesting i/o are put temporarily into the *wait state,* while the cpu executes another program and the channel completes the i/o. The *job scheduler* program decides which programs should be taken off disk and loaded into core to participate in multiprogramming, or *concurrent execution.*

Before the job can execute, however, it must be converted from the source language in which it is written to the *machine language* that the CPU can execute. A *language translator* program executes to perform this function (language translators will be described in Chapter 8).

Eventually, the *processor scheduler* or *dispatcher* sets up the program to run, and the CPU executes it. When the program requests I/O, it goes into the wait state while the I/O *traffic controller* handles its request and the dispatcher sets up and runs another job. When the I/O request is finished, this program becomes "ready to run" again. It waits for the dispatcher to select it from the waiting group, or *queue,* of ready programs. Eventually, the program is completed. This means that either it has run to successful completion or it has been stopped because of unacceptable error condition, called *abnormal termination.* In either case, it and certain completion information are taken off the CPU and *spooled* to disk. Finally, the spooler program transfers the data to the printer, where it is printed, and the job is finished.

Figure 31 schematically depicts the various transitions involved in a job's life cycle. Note that the program may be revolved through the "I/O triangle" many times for various input/output requests before actually completing and leaving the system.

A word of caution is necessary about this description. Remember that it is only a general and simplified model of the ways in which the operating system interacts with a job during its life process. It distinguishes the major parts of the monitor program and what they do; most important, it gives an indication as to the operating system's purposes. The operating system aids the program through the system, providing services that system users might not be able to program themselves. At the same time, it monitors the entire system's operation, attempting to achieve the most efficient management of limited system resources.

One additional comment on the life process description: Remember that the CPU is executing only a single instruction in a single program at any one time. The operating system syn-

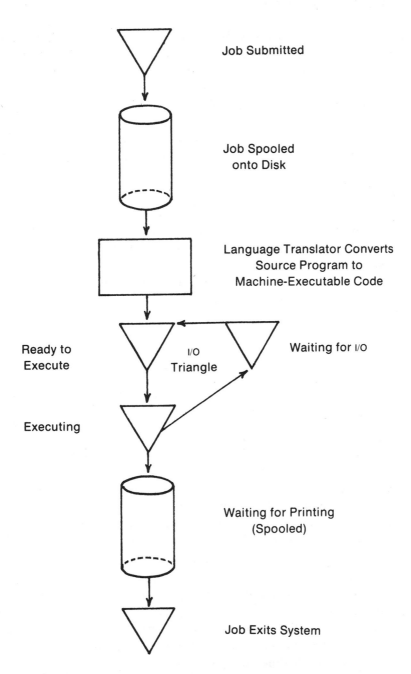

Figure 31 THE LIFE CYCLE OF A TYPICAL JOB.

chronizes all of the running programs to ensure that everything occurs in the proper sequence at the proper moment by controlling
timing and the order in which functions are accomplished and programs are run.

Finally, note that a job submitted to the system may involve
more than one *step*. A *job step* corresponds to a single program's execution. In a multistep job, programs are run one after another in
the order in which they appear in the job (see Figure 32). When the
job is in the computer system, program A will be run to completion,
then program B, and then program C. The job will be completed
only when the last step, program C, is finished. In Figure 32, note
that only program A has data in the card deck. If the other programs
use data, they will be reading it from other sources, perhaps from
the storage medium devices discussed in Chapter 4. In addition,
the job shown in Figure 32 could exist on disk, instead of on computer cards, and could be read in and executed from there.

RESOURCE MANAGEMENT VIEW

The reader has taken an oversimplified tour of the operating system
by following a job in process; the operating system program now
will be examined in terms of resource management. Jobs may
come into the system more or less continuously, each requesting
resources and desiring to run on the system's single CPU. The
operating system must coordinate all of the tasks the system will
perform, synchronize the timing of operations, and ensure that
programs will be executed in an orderly manner. In effect, for each
resource the system has, the control program must determine who
gets it, how, and when. It must allocate and reclaim the resource
from the individual programs. At all times, the operating system
must be able to check the status of every resource of the computer
system.

Resources of the computing system may be divided into four
categories. *Processor management* is concerned with efficient use of the
CPU. The job scheduler decides which programs to allow on the
system and into core memory for eligibility to run under

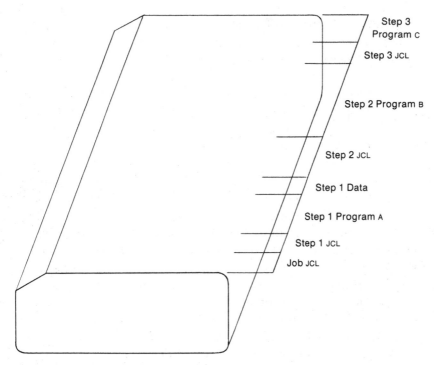

Figure 32 PROCESSING A MULTISTEP JOB.

multiprogramming. The process scheduler or dispatcher decides which program the CPU should execute at any one time and sets up this program on the CPU. Generally, the traffic controller is in charge of checking the status of individual programs and coordinating the scheduling. A primary objective of processor management is to keep the CPU busy at all times, which is effective CPU *utilization*. Multiprogramming systems ensure that the CPU is not sitting idle while a slow I/O operation takes place. Instead, in a multiprogramming operating system, the CPU is set up to go to another program. It can return to running the slow program at a later time, after another job has been completed. The channel processor(s) will relieve the fast CPU from overseeing the tedious I/O operation.

I/O *device management* is responsible for the proper use and allocation of all system printers, card readers, tape drives, disk drives, CRTs, and other system devices. The I/O traffic controller program generally is in charge of policing I/O allocation and reclamation. The I/O *scheduler* readies a channel for performing an I/O task, and I/O *device handlers* manipulate I/O particulars for specific device types.

I/O device management can be very complicated, because of the distinction between *dedicated* and *shared* devices. Dedicated devices must be allocated to a single program for the duration of that program's execution. A printer, for example, can be used only by a single program at any one time. If two or more programs were permitted to use it concurrently, their outputs would be intermingled. Clearly, such intermixed output from several programs would be of little value.

Shared devices are those I/O devices that can be used by many different programs, without having to wait for the termination of one program before being assigned to the next one. Disk drives are an example; their access arms can move in and out, and since the files for different programs are located in different places on the disk pack, intermixing the output incorrectly cannot occur.

Device virtualization is a technique used in the more sophisticated operating systems to make a dedicated device look like a shared device to any executing program. This technique enhances system efficiency, because shared devices can be used by many programs running in parallel. They need not be assigned to a single program for the duration of that program's execution. Note that as programs perform I/O operations, they traverse the I/O triangle of Figure 31. So it is possible that many programs may want a dedicated device concurrently.

How does virtualization work? Instead of writing a program's output directly to the printer (a necessarily dedicated device), the operating system can have programs write their printer outputs to a disk. The disk is a shared device, which can be used concurrently by many programs. Meanwhile, the spooler program writes output from the disk to the dedicated printer. It selects output on the disk only from completed programs; therefore, complete output reports are written correctly on the printer, one after another. This technique is called *device virtualization*, or *spooling*, and is one of the marks of a "good" operating system, because system efficiency is increased.

File management is another aspect of the operating system's resource management. Files—the datasets or groups of logical records discussed in Chapter 3—are managed by the JCL *monitor* program. The JCL monitor program ensures that a program will have access to the data files it needs when its turn arrives for execution.

Main memory is the final major resource the operating system must control. In Chapter 1, main memory was defined as that memory which is accessed solely electronically. Core memory is where programs must reside in order to execute. This concept is distinct from the various storage mediums discussed in Chapter 4, which required physical I/O device movement in order to have their data accessed. Data access through I/O devices is significantly slower than direct access to data residing in main memory.

The amount of main memory tends to be a limiting factor on the power of many computing systems and accounts for much of the expense. Memory management schemes are indicative of the sophistication and effectiveness of both the operating system program and the computing system as a whole; therefore, they will be discussed at length in Chapter 6.

Finally, it should be mentioned that some books on this topic include the language translators (programming languages) as a part of operating system discussions. In the author's opinion, this is not appropriate, because the language translators form part of the systems support software. Programming languages are an extremely important topic in relation to library computing systems. Why this is so, and a specific evaluation of different programming languages for library programming needs, deserve the extensive discussion to be found in Chapter 8.

EVALUATION OF OPERATING SYSTEMS

Operating systems are highly complex computer programs. The complexity and subtlety of operating systems relate directly to the distinction made between systems and applications programmers in Chapter 2. The applications programmer knows how to interact with the operating system in order to run specific programs on the system. Applications programmers are not normally apprised of the many intricacies of the internal mechanisms occurring in the operating system. Systems programmers are more aware of how the operating system executes; often they are involved with measuring system efficiency and fine-tuning certain variable aspects of the operating system's performance. They are responsible for upgrading system performance and installing and testing any program packages added to the operating system or system support software.

It is possible to gauge an entire computer system's effectiveness and performance by certain measurements. CPU *utilization,* for instance, can be measured and analyzed with software packages by the system programmer. *Turnaround time* is the elapsed time between the submission of a job to the system and the time when it is completed and printed. Librarians and others should seek the following from a system: Is the average turnaround time very good? Is there a notion of "guaranteed turnaround time?" Do some lower priority jobs take days to get out of the system? Is it possible to communicate the relative priority of a job to the operating system? And is it possible to get a high-priority job through the system quickly?

There is also a general measurement called *throughput,* which measures the work capacity (by the number of jobs of specific size and characteristics) that the system can run and turn around within a period of time. What sort of throughput does a system achieve each day? Exactly how was that throughput measured?

The functions that an operating system offers are a measure of its general effectiveness and overall "goodness." Some systems achieve these functions with less operating system overhead than others. In some situations, a more limited operating system may be desirable; in others, the full extent and range of functions provided is more desirable. In the final analysis, the ratio of function to simplicity may be an accurate formula for conceptualizing the relative merits of operating systems software.

CHAPTER 6

Memory Management

Memory management is one of the most important software functions of the operating system. In many computing systems, main memory is one of the more expensive and limiting resources. Memory constraints often impose more severe limitations on a system's capabilities than any other system resource factor.

For these reasons, memory management traditionally has been the focus of much of the evolution and development in operating systems programs. Consequently, memory management is one area of software development where quantitative and rapid progress has been made.

Methods of memory management are a distinguishing feature of operating systems. When a brief description of an operating system is requested, the most likely response will be a direct reference to the operating system's memory management scheme. In addition to the fact that memory management techniques often are a valid way of classifying the relative sophistication of a computing system's software, memory management methods usually are correlated directly with the relative power of the computing system. A distinctive characteristic between mainframes, minicomputers, and microcomputers is found in their memory management techniques. Memory management is an excellent indication of the computing system's size and power, and the topic is related closely to certain key concepts of which all computer users should be aware. Multiprogramming is of great relevance here, because the concurrent execution of programs is fundamental to the operation of any modern mainframe. Perhaps the major computer concept implemented in the 1970s is *virtual storage,* another memory management concept.

In this chapter, memory management methodologies will be approached in the order of increasingly sophisticated and efficient memory management systems. These systems fit into a historical pattern of evolution in mainframe development. The simplest and most primitive methods, which are discussed first, are obsolete only in details of mainframe development; they still enjoy widespread use—in mini- and microcomputer operating systems.

ADDRESSABILITY

The topic of memory management is dependent on the concept of addressability. Core memory is divided uniformly into bytes and words, as defined in Chapter 1. Thus, everything that exists in computer memory has an *address,* which is simply a numerical reference to the location in memory where that item exists. Figure 33 shows how a computer program might be stored in memory. The program itself, that is, instructions that will be executed by the computer, takes up memory space and has addresses for all of

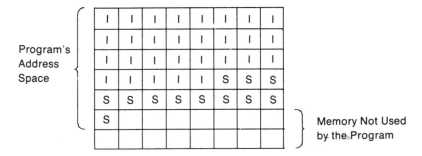

I = Space Occupied by Program's Instructions
S = Storage Space Reserved for Program's Use

Figure 33   A PROGRAM STORED IN MEMORY.

the pertinent locations in core. Associated with the program is its reserved storage space. It would be here, for example, that the program would read a record off a tape into core. The program could give the CPU instructions to read in the record, and by means of addressability, the program would tell where to place the data record in memory. Each box in Figure 33, called a *memory location*, has a unique address associated with it. The sum of the program's instructions and data space is called that program's *address space*. If the program tried to address a location outside of its reserved address space, then it is making an error. Computer hardware would detect this errant addressing by the program, and the program would be stopped on the basis of a *protection error*. What if the user program accidentally addresses a location where the operating system resides and tries to read a record into that space? Through analysis of the reasonability of addresses a program might refer to, the computer system has a method of guaranteeing *protection* against errant addressing to ensure the system's integrity.

The computer hardware can detect a program-addressing error through a system of *locks* and *keys*. A program has an associated key, which is a numerical value automatically set at the time the program is loaded into memory. Each memory location of Figure 33 has an associated lock. The program's key fits only locks in its address space. When it tries to access anywhere else, the computer hardware automatically stops the program for the protection error and turns control over to the operating system program. The hardware mechanism that gives control over to the operating system is an *interrupt*. The operating system is brought back onto the CPU by the interrupt mechanism; in this way, the operating system can always regain control of the computer's operations.

UNIPROGRAMMING MEMORY MANAGEMENT

A uniprogramming computing system represents the simplest form of computer operating system. In a uniprogramming system, a single program is brought into core and executed through to completion.

Figure 34 illustrates such a system. A single program resides in memory until it has finished executing. Meanwhile, the operating system itself is always in memory. It is there ready to execute should the interrupt mechanism start it, due to an error in the user program.

The advantages of this system of memory management are:

1. Simplicity. The operating system program may be very simple, and, as a result, the system is easy for its operators to use and understand.

2. Due to its simplicity, the operating system program may use very little space, for instance, a few kilobytes. In a small computer, this is ideal, since little space is available for the operating system. This is in contrast to more sophisticated operating systems, which often may require 256 to 512 kilobytes of memory.

3. Protection is simplified. The operating system is a "permanent" program, and it may exist on a form of memory called *read*

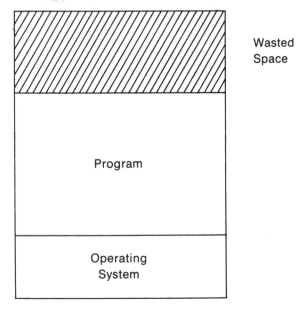

Figure 34   THE MEMORY MANAGEMENT FUNCTION IN A
UNIPROGRAMMING SYSTEM.

only memory, or ROM. Because this memory cannot be written on, due to its hardware nature, the operating system does not need locks and keys to protect its own integrity. This is how most microcomputers and some minicomputers implement protection principles.

Disadvantages of this system of memory management may be summarized as:

1. Any memory not used by the single program loaded into memory is wasted.
2. There is no multiprogramming, since only one program in core is ready to run at a time. Therefore, the CPU is vastly underutilized, wasting much of its time as tedious I/O operations are performed. This results in serious degradation of the work load that the CPU can perform over a given period of time; however, it does have the result that channels are not necessary.

It is obvious that uniprogramming is found only in primitive or very small operating systems. The mainframes of the 1950s did, in fact, work in this way before modern computing concepts were developed. Today, mainframes that use the uniprogramming approach to memory management are most definitely obsolete. But for the microcomputers invented during the mid-1970s, uniprogramming was a perfect approach. These systems had up to 64K in maximum memory and usually had even less in typical systems configurations. Their main appeal was low price. CPU utilization and throughput were not considerations in microcomputers. Microcomputers and their possibilities for the library world will be discussed at length in Chapter 11. In summary, it is clear that uniprogramming has a definite place in the computing world, but only with the smallest systems.

STATIC-PARTITION MULTIPROGRAMMING

This is the earliest form of memory management offering multiprogramming. The advantages of multiprogramming have already been discussed, but the reader should remember that CPU utilization is the primary goal. Since the CPU does the work of executing programs, keeping it optimally busy greatly improves the system's productivity.

Figure 35 shows a computer system's main memory, divided into fixed-size blocks called *partitions*. As jobs are entered into the system, the operating system checks to see if any partitions are not being used. If so, it will place the job into the partition closest in size to that of the job's address space. Figure 36 gives an example of how jobs simultaneously in core may look with this system—any space within a partition that a job does not actually need or use is wasted.

The best advantage of a static-partition memory management system is that it provides for multiprogramming. It logically follows that the more partitions the system has, the greater the degree of multiprogramming; maximizing the extent of multiprogramming tends to maximize CPU utilization and system

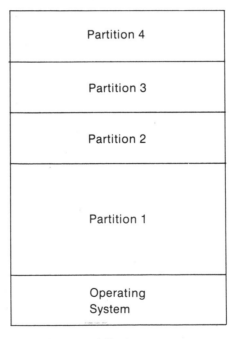

Figure 35   A MEMORY MANAGEMENT SYSTEM USING STATIC PARTITIONS.

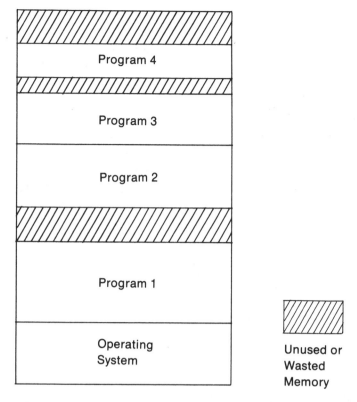

Figure 36   PROGRAMS LOADED INTO MEMORY IN A STATIC-PARTITION MEMORY MANAGEMENT SYSTEM.

throughput. But the limit on the extent of memory partitioning is that jobs will not be able to fit into partitions that are too small.

The disadvantage to static partitions is that some memory in each partition may remain unused. Having such wasted pieces of core is called *memory fragmentation* or *fragmentation*.

An important feature among static-partition systems concerns the permanency of partition size. In earlier systems, the partition size was built into the operating system. More sophisticated systems allow for partitions to be altered by the operator with varying degrees of ease. With many modern systems, changing partition size takes only a few minutes. This is a very significant feature, because foreknowledge of jobs to be submitted to the system and their sizes can be used to adjust to the most appropriate partition sizes.

Since the mid-1960s, IBM has used static-partition memory management as part of one of the operating systems offered for the Series 360 computers. This operating system is called the *disk operating system* (DOS). Although it may not be strictly accurate, many people in programming and the computer industry refer to operating systems with static partitions as DOS systems.

The DOS approach to memory allocation, in various forms, was quite popular for mainframes in the 1960s. Many mainframes still have this form of memory management, although it is often combined with other, more advanced concepts that will be discussed later. With or without various modifications, static-partition memory management is now extremely popular for minicomputers. Most minicomputer systems have procedures for quickly and easily altering partition sizes. When the job size is known in advance, or where job size is fairly consistent, static partitions work very well.

Generally, static partitions are not so efficient when requirements for jobs coming into the system vary widely. Flexibility in fixing partitions usually is offered, but only through operator intervention.

Another objection to static partitions is that there are small pieces of unused core in different partitions. Memory fragmentation is a problem because a larger contiguous piece could be large enough to fit another program into memory.

Both of these shortcomings of static-partition memory management can be resolved by using other methodologies. The solution to the former problem is addressed in the scheme to be described next.

DYNAMIC-PARTITION MEMORY MANAGEMENT

In this approach to memory management, partitions or *regions* are under the flexible control of the operating system. Regions are allocated to match program size as programs come into the system. If, at any time, unallocated portions of memory are contiguous to one another, they are automatically coalesced into single, larger, more useful pieces of core. Thus, the system responds dynamically to the stream of job needs for memory as programs are submitted.

Figure 37 shows a *job stream*—a group of jobs as they are submitted to the computing system—and illustrates how dynamic memory management responds as these jobs enter the system. Note especially how free space from programs 1 and 2 was coalesced to form a larger contiguous block of memory, after both jobs had left the system, in Frame 5. On the other hand, the system lacks any ability to change the location of memory fragments within core. Frame 4 shows two such fragments that could not be coalesced into one fragment because they were not adjacent to one another.

Advantages to this method of dynamically allocated regions include:

1. All of the advantages previously listed under static partitioning.

2. It is much more responsive and flexible to the varying needs of incoming programs than static partitioning. Although static partitions can be altered only at the speed of operator intervention, dynamic memory management allows a computer to do this.

3. Adjacent core fragments can be combined and made into larger, more useful blocks of memory.

Shortcomings are:

1. Fragmentation still occurs because noncontiguous free space cannot be combined.

2. At this point in operating system development, the size of the operating system has become quite large. Substantial core will be required for the operating system.

Some distinguishing characteristics between systems using dynamic memory management are:

1. The size of the operating system needed for implementation.

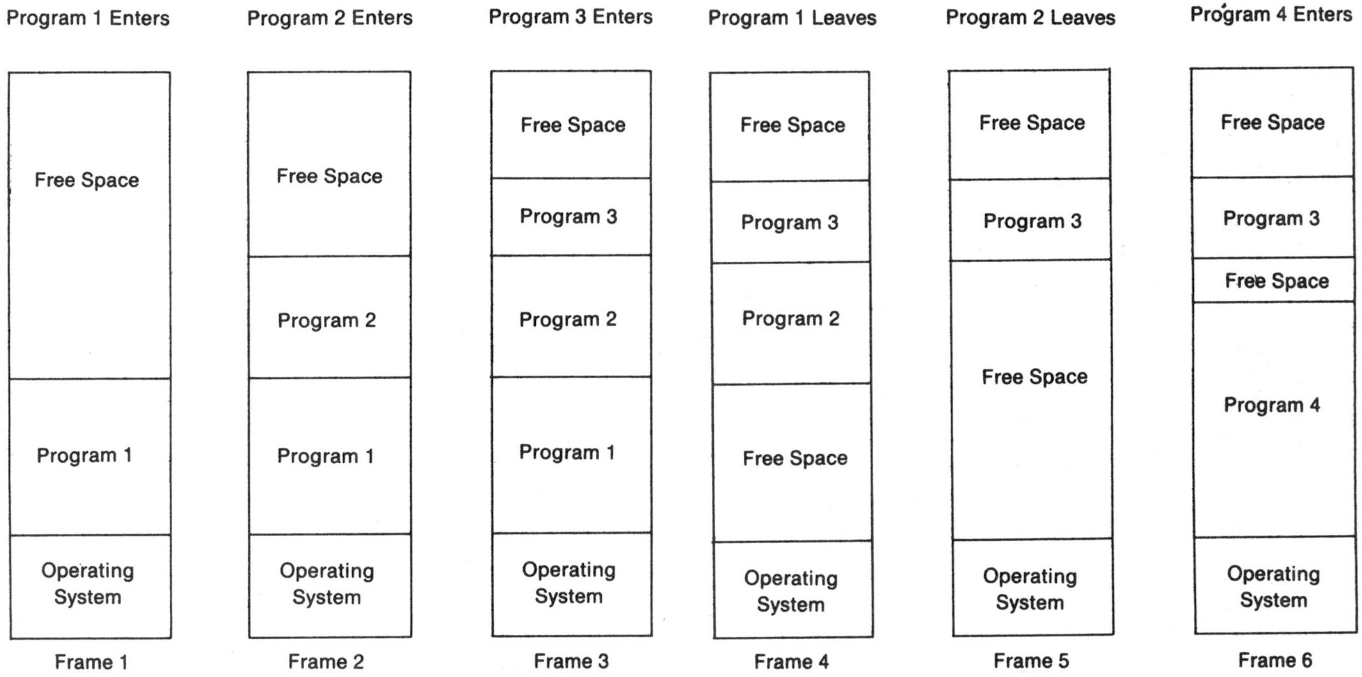

Figure 37 MEMORY MANAGEMENT BY DYNAMIC PARTITIONING.

2. The actual methodologies used in deciding which free block of core to allocate to a new program, provided there is more than one place available. The nature of these techniques is beyond the scope of this book, but they can have an appreciable effect on the efficiency of dynamic partitioning systems.

3. The presence or absence of the *roll-in/roll-out* feature. With this feature, a program may be rolled out of core and stored on disk in order to provide enough contiguous room for a higher priority job. After the higher priority program is finished, the original program may be rolled back into its old position in core. This technique adds fluidity to memory management and can be useful if properly implemented. Static partitioning may offer roll-in/roll-out as well.

Dynamic memory management was an extremely popular approach in computer systems during the 1960s and 1970s for medium and large computers. For minicomputers, it usually was not used as often as DOS, its variants, and the relocatable systems to be discussed, because of the core space requirement for the operating system itself.

PROGRAM RELOCATION MEMORY MANAGEMENT

All of the memory management systems already outlined have one important shortcoming. They are vulnerable to core fragmentation, which results in unused or wasted memory space. Dynamic partitioning came closest to resolving this problem, through its dynamic response to job sizes encountered in the job stream and its ability to combine adjacent core fragments into single larger pieces.

The obvious solution to fragmentation is to stop program execution and to relocate all programs in the system to contiguous positions in core; then, all unused core could be coalesced into a single, more usable section of memory. This process could be performed whenever a new job enters the system, at random intervals, or whenever a new job that enters the system will be able to fit into memory only if programs currently in core undergo relocation. In any case, the last alternative is the most attractive.

This relocation process, called memory *compaction, recompaction,* or *burping the memory,* is illustrated in Figure 38. After the relocation process occurs, core fragments are grouped into a single section of memory.

The main difficulty associated with relocating to further multiprogramming is that many instructions in a program refer to various places within that program's address space: This is the concept of addressability explained earlier. After the job is moved in the system's memory, these addresses become incorrect. In a

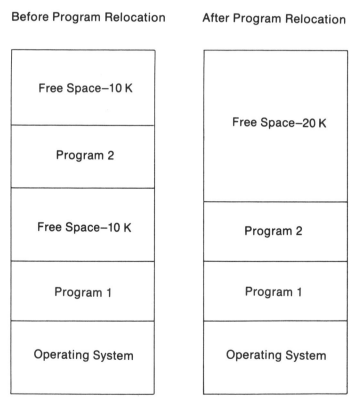

Before Program Relocation | After Program Relocation

Before Program Relocation	After Program Relocation
Free Space—10 K	Free Space—20 K
Program 2	
Free Space—10 K	Program 2
Program 1	Program 1
Operating System	Operating System

Figure 38   PROGRAM RELOCATION AS A FORM OF MEMORY MANAGEMENT.

static- or dynamic-partition system, all addresses are adjusted correctly when the program is first *loaded* into memory; however, if a job is moved, they become inaccurate.

This addressability dilemma is resolved by the technique of *dynamic address translation,* or DAT. In dynamic address translation, before any program instruction is executed by the CPU, any address (or addresses) in that instruction is relocated by adding to it a value appropriate to the present position of the program's present address space in memory. The *base relocation register,* or *relocation register,* contains the value to reflect current program location.

Protection may be implemented by comparing each address, after DAT, to a value in the *bounds register.* The bounds register is set to indicate the highest value any address may have in a given program. Protection for addresses lower than those in the program is achieved through the relocation register. Thus, relocatable memory partitioning leads to a convenient protection scheme as well as to a solution of the fragmentation problem.

In general, advantages of relocatable partitions are:

1. A job that might not get into memory due to fragmentation in the previously discussed systems will be loaded into core by this system after compaction occurs.

2. Fragmentation is eliminated as a memory management problem. This leads to a greater extent of multiprogramming, with its associated benefits of better memory and CPU utilization.

3. Although this is a very different approach from the approaches discussed earlier, it is no more complex and certainly as valid as the other methods.

Important disadvantages are:

1. Time expended on movement of programs is considerable when compaction occurs.

2. Dynamic address translation is an overhead expense that is necessary for execution of almost all instructions. This, however, usually slows down execution very slightly.

3. There is the added cost of relocation hardware.

Altogether, the relocatable partition approach to memory management is a valuable technology. For minicomputers, particularly, it has been used with great success, but for mainframes, it never achieved much popularity due to the advent of virtual storage systems.

PAGING SYSTEMS

Another solution to the memory fragmentation problem is *paged memory management,* or *paging.* This solution eliminates a basic restrictive assumption common to all the systems mentioned. This assumption is that a program's entire address space must consist of a single block of contiguous memory.

In paged memory management, a program's address space is divided into small, uniformly sized units. In most computing systems, these units are either two or four kilobyte *pages.* Figure 39 depicts this situation.

Main memory also is divided into equivalent-size sections called *blocks,* as shown in Figure 40. The operating system does not need to be divided into blocks and pages, since it does not participate in the paging process. It is always resident in a single area of core memory.

Program Address Space	A	B	C	D
	E	F	G	H
	I	J	K	L

Figure 39   A PROGRAM DIVIDED INTO PAGES.

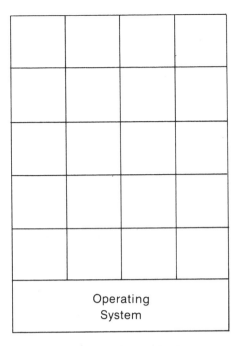

Figure 40   MEMORY DIVIDED INTO BLOCKS.

Program loading consists of loading a program's pages into the memory blocks of core. The pages need not be contiguous in core, as Figure 41 illustrates. Meanwhile, two sets of tables are maintained by the operating system. The *page map tables*—one for each job loaded into memory—record where the pages for a program are loaded in core; the *memory block tables* keep track of the status of each memory block in the system. Therefore, the operating system knows which blocks are or are not currently in use.

The main advantage to this paging system is that it eliminates the need for all of a program's address space to be contiguous in core. As seen from the systems already described, this can be a very limiting restriction. Thus, paged memory management provides an answer to the core fragmentation problem without getting involved in the sort of physical movement of partitions that relocatable memory management requires. The time consumed in relocating programs is saved time.

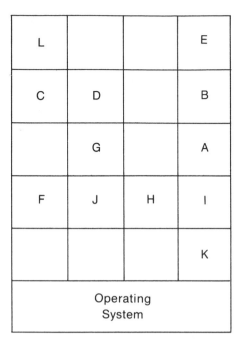

Figure 41   PROGRAM PAGES PLACED INTO MEMORY BLOCKS.

The drawback of paged memory management is the memory and processor overhead expense involved in the maintenance of page and memory block tables. There must be one page table per program in the system, while only one memory block table needs to be maintained by the operating system.

VIRTUAL STORAGE

The paging concept has been implemented as the memory management methodology for some systems. Only a short conceptual jump is required to achieve virtual storage, and, in actuality, the paging method just described is not widely used.

To introduce the virtual storage concept, one question is appropriate. Is there any reason that all the pages of a program must exist in core at exactly the same time? Since the CPU actually performs only one instruction at a time, the number of pages needed in core for a program's execution is likely to be minimal at any given time. When there is a need to refer to a page not in core, a hardware *interrupt* can notify the CPU of this event; then the operating system can load the needed page into memory. The operating system program can return control to the subject program, and it can resume its execution as if the necessary page had always been in memory.

Now that the basic concept of virtual memory has been introduced, a fuller explanation will be provided. The idea, again, is to give the computer's operating system a method of memory management that allows the system to act as if it has more memory than it really does. Thus, memory is "virtualized" or extended by software methods.

When a typical program enters the system, it is written into a DASD storage area referred to as the *page set*. The page set contains copies of all address spaces of programs currently on the system. A few pages of the program are loaded into actual core or *real memory*; they will be the pages required to initiate execution of this program. Then, the program is run in the normal manner of concurrent execution or multiprogramming. Since this is a paging system, the regular procedures of dynamic address translation are followed for addresses encountered in the program's instructions. In other words, page map and memory block tables are used for paging. But each page reference in the page map tables also contains an extra indicator that tells if that page is actually in core or if it is only in the page set on disk. The system uses this indicator during DAT to locate any needed page of the program.

As the program executes, if a page needed for continued execution is not in core memory, this situation will be recognized during dynamic address translation. A *page interrupt* notifies the operating system, the operating system loads the appropriate page into real memory, control is returned back to the subject program, and the user program resumes its running as if no *paging operation* had been required.

While the *demand paging* system is operating, a situation will develop where there is no free memory block into which to load a page. A page interrupt will occur, and there will be no open memory block into which the page from the page set can be loaded into core. The system must decide which page, possibly of another program, to put back on the page set disk. This vacated memory block will be used to load the required page into core.

Theoretically, it would be desirable if the system could replace a page that will not be used or referred to again in the near future. The most desirable solution would be achieved if the system could replace a page that would never be used again.

Such an ideal solution is impossible to implement in a computer operating system program without prescience. But a technique has been developed that can estimate which page is least likely to be reused in the near future.

The *least recently used* (LRU) solution proposes that the system keep track of which pages in memory were used recently and which were not. By statistical measuring of program execution patterns, it has been established that there is a correlation between a program's not having needed a given page in core recently and its probable tendency not to need this same page again in the near future.

The least recently used rule is a technique that allows for selection of a memory block into which to bring a needed page when no free block exists. It predicts which page can be put back on the page set with the least likelihood of being *demand paged* into memory in the near future. Therefore, the needed page can be brought into memory with the least amount of work to the system. If the memory block selected for the paging operation contains a page that has not been altered since being loaded, this page does not need to be written back on the paging set itself. It was copied there originally, when its program first came into the system. Unless altered, it exists on the page set disk and does not need to be written again.

At this point, the life cycle of a program run under a demand paged or virtual memory management system will be reviewed. As the program is selected for multiprogramming, it is written on the page disk for inclusion in the page set. The program is not loaded directly into core, as would have been done in the systems of memory management previously described. Only the first few pages of the program are loaded into real memory to allow the program to begin execution. The program can now take its normal turn in running under a multiprogramming system. Dynamic address translation is used for making the paged memory management method work. DAT allows the program to execute as though it were a single contiguous block of address space in memory, even though it is actually disparate pages in core. Dynamic address translation will recognize whether a page needed for execution at some time is not in memory but only on the page set disk. In this case, a *page fault* occurs, and the page interrupt mechanism will load the needed page into core. If there is no free memory block available, the least recently used rule provides a method to determine which page to page out of core in order to provide a memory block into which to copy the needed page. After the paging process is completed, control is returned to the subject program. It now continues its execution.

From this description of virtual memory systems, it can be seen that there is much software overhead involved in such a system. The system must maintain the page map and memory block tables. In addition, it must update information about pages least recently referenced and, also, those that have been changed in any way since being admitted into real memory. There are many finer points of system overhead not mentioned in the conceptual presentation given here, the worst of which is that it is possible that page interrupts might occur constantly. In such a situation, the CPU would have to operate the memory management system, spending all of its time copying pages in and out of core from the page set. This condition is called *thrashing*. When thrashing occurs, the CPU's time is totally devoted to running the memory management system—demand paging—rather than working on the jobs submitted to the system. A *thrashing monitor* program is added to the operating system to ensure that the virtual memory system does not run awry.

Although software overhead is involved in virtual memory systems, there are other principles that help them operate efficiently. The least recently used rule is one. The LRU principle allows for a method of estimating which pages currently in core need not be there in the future. As page interrupts occur, memory blocks to be involved in the paging process are selected so as to hold down the number of future paging operations required.

Also, over a period of time, certain pages of a program will be used frequently and, therefore, will remain in core; this is the *working set* of the program. The working set is only a part of the program's total address space, and, once it is in memory, the program will tend to operate efficiently under virtual memory management.

Why is only a portion of any program needed in memory at any time? The principle of *locality of reference* states that certain instructions in a program will tend to be executed again and again. These are *programming loops*—commonly seen patterns in computer programs. Furthermore, particular parts of programs may be executed or referenced very infrequently, if at all. For example, a program's error routines usually will not be needed. Virtual memory management allows the error routines to remain on the page set disk instead of actually occupying valuable core memory. But, if they are needed, they will be loaded through the page interrupt process. Finally, different sections of programs tend to be executed at mutually exclusive times. This, again, relates to the basic nature of programming and the logical structures of programs.

All of these principles, inherent in the nature of programs and their logical constructs, are recognized and maximized by demand paged memory management. The parts or pages of programs that often are needed in the program's execution will tend to remain in the working set and exist in core memory. Other pages will remain in the page set, to be loaded into primary memory as necessary. All programs exist in their totality only on disk in the page set. Initial loading of programs into memory in a virtual memory management system is accomplished here only by including them in the disk page set. Since virtual memory on disk is larger than real memory or core, in a sense, disk is being used to expand the size of core memory, hence, the name "virtual" storage and the basic principle of all virtual memory systems. Less expensive disk storage can be used to reduce demands on real memory, and the computing system operates as if it has more memory than it actually has. The principles involved in the working set concept help this method to operate with reasonable efficiency.

To list the general advantages of virtual storage, it should be noted that:

1. The system acts as if it has more real memory than it actually has. Due to this virtualization of memory, more programs can be executing at one time. Multiprogramming is increased to a greater extent than was possible without virtual memory. The ultimate goals of processor and memory utilization are similarly aided.

2. Virtual memory is larger than real system memory. The concept of memory hierarchies is used to substitute less expensive disk storage for real memory to create the larger virtual storage. A benefit of this virtualization of storage, for example, is that a program too large for the computing system's memory now can be run on that system.

3. Fragmentation of storage has been solved without physically relocating entire programs. Pages of a program are not required to be physically contiguous in core. Memory is used efficiently in other ways as well: Unused parts of programs do not take up memory, and portions of programs used only once or infrequently will require memory space only when they are actually referenced. The least recently used method thus guarantees efficient use of memory.

Disadvantages to virtual storage include:

1. The software overhead involved in keeping page map and memory block tables updated; keeping the status of changed and least recently used pages current; and calling the pages in and out of real memory.

2. The extra memory required for the tables and the software and memory overhead needed for the system to operate. Again, these tables are for keeping track of the status of programs and their pages and memory blocks.

3. Hardware and processing costs represented by features such

as page interrupts and dynamic address translation. Additional hardware features not discussed here generally are needed to maintain system efficiency, due to the large amount of software overhead involved in demand paging.

4. A thrashing monitor must be added to the operating system to prevent useless thrashing by the system.

5. Pages must be of an appropriate size. If they are too small, thrashing will occur. If they are too large, a small amount of memory will be wasted through the phenomenon of *internal page fragmentation*. Since thrashing renders the computer system useless, the latter usually occurs.

In general, virtual storage memory management is the most advanced method for large computing systems. These systems have enough space in their operating systems for the degree of sophistication and memory and software overhead required. Also, hardware costs required for virtual storage are distributed better across the cost of the larger computing system.

Large computers using forms of demand paging include the IBM System 370 and the Honeywell 6180. The former uses page sizes of either two or four kilobytes.

The ratio of virtual memory to real memory for these systems is variable. The thrashing monitors and the operators (under the direction of systems programmers) serve to define this ratio. In normal operation, ratios ranging from 1.5–2.0 virtual memory to 1.0 real memory are common. Therefore, in many cases, virtual storage can effectively double the memory capacity of a computing system.

Current IBM operating systems offering virtual storage include DOS/VSE and OS/VS2 Release 2. IBM released its first virtual storage operating system for general sale in 1972. An interesting fact about virtual memory systems is that they were pioneered in Britain as early as 1960.[1] It was only with IBM's adoption of these

---

[1] The concept of paging developed in the Atlas system is summarized in J. Fotheringham, "Dynamic Storage Allocation in the Atlas Computer Including an Automatic Use of a Backing Store," *Communications of the Association for Computing Machinery,* 4(10):435–435, October 1961.

principles in the early 1970s, however, that virtual storage systems were marketed on a large scale.

Due to the large software operating system overhead involved, minicomputers generally do not use virtual storage. Advances in hardware and software technologies develop so rapidly, however, that such minicomputers as those manufactured by Prime, DEC, Wang, and others are operating effectively with forms of virtual storage memory management. About the only prediction that can be made with certainty is that such advances will continue to occur.

SUMMARY

In this chapter, various methods of memory management by the operating system have been discussed. They have been presented in a sequence of conceptual development, with particular emphasis on the general advantages and disadvantages of differing approaches to the problem. Some evaluations were made of those methods that are appropriate to computing systems of varying sizes, given the current state of technology and the computing market.

The reader is urged to look at Appendix C, which provides figures diagramming the development of the operating systems marketed by IBM. These figures serve to reinforce the general conceptual picture and also to reemphasize the fact that the distinguishing feature of many operating systems is their form of memory management.

Memory management has been described in detail for library employees who, as intelligent computer users, must be aware of the major concepts and differences involved in various memory management systems. Too often, terms and concepts such as multiprogramming and virtual storage remain obtuse or mysterious to computer users who need to understand them and their implications.

CHAPTER 7

Systems Support Software

As previously defined, an operating system is a computer program whose purposes are to promote efficiency and to make the computer more serviceable to its programmers. Thus, the operating system is a single program that controls and directs use of the computing system's resources.

The term "operating system," however, sometimes is also used in the broader sense of referring to all the internal or service programs in the computer system. Like the operating system program itself, these other systems programs promote efficient and convenient use of the computer system. And, like the operating system, these programs are written to perform with a particular manufacturer's computer system and its hardware architecture.

In this book, the auxiliary service programs will be referred to as "systems support software." The main goal of systems support software is to make it easier for programmers to use the computer. The systems programs provide a means of accomplishing tasks that are performed routinely at an installation but would be quite difficult to achieve without ready-made programs.

Access methods, mentioned in Chapter 3, are a good example of support software. These general-purpose programs provide I/O support for user programs. They perform the many device-dependent and extremely detailed aspects of input/output with which few programmers are conversant. Since it may be assumed that all purchasers of a computer will be doing input/output, the manufacturer of a computer will sell access-method software as an integral part of the computer system. This is more economical and practical for all concerned than it would be for each purchaser to attempt to write reliable access methods.

Certain systems support programs also may be purchased or rented by computer users from companies other than the computer manufacturer. *Software vendors* are organizations that specialize in the creation and support of systems support software for computer equipment made by other companies. Database systems, described in Chapter 10, are an example of such "add on" systems support software produced and marketed by software vendors.

Obviously, systems support programs are fundamental to the usability and power of any computing system. Librarians and administrators in libraries need to have a general understanding of the nature of these programs and their purposes. This chapter focuses on support software programs relevant to library systems requirements.

UTILITIES

Utilities are general-purpose programs provided in the system to manage or manipulate its data files. Utility programs may perform operations such as copying or listing files, compressing datasets on disk (compacting disk storage), creating backup files, readying files for *export* or transfer to another computer system, and sorting files; others might create sample test data or attempt to verify the accuracy of backup copies of files; and some provide services that are specific to the computing system on which they run. Most utilities are executed either through particular job control language statements or by other specific commands given to the operating system program.

One class of utility programs—those intended for data copying— performs services such as moving data files to different locations on disk, creating backup files, copying files to different storage mediums, and listing or dumping file data on the printer. *Disk compression* utilities, for example, which are included in this group of utilities, copy files into contiguous disk locations. Disk compression programs are an example of programs that are not provided with all computing systems but that may be purchased separately at a later date.

The important aspects of copying and moving utilities are the mediums they involve, the types of data they handle, and their actual purposes. Among copy utilities, for example, some copy from tape to disk and vice versa, while others copy from disk or tape to the printer; some destroy the original files, but most do not. Some copy utilities may do any of these tasks, depending on the commands they are given.

There are some utilities that operate only on ASCII or EBCDIC files or on binary files; others operate on any data. What does the library do when it has only a copy utility for EBCDIC files and it wants to copy an ASCII tape? This type of problem points out the importance of having the proper utilities for particular situations.

Usually, vendors tend to write general-purpose utility programs, in which event one or two general utilities may be capable of any of the previously mentioned tasks. Other manufacturers will create narrower programs by providing a different utility for each of many different purposes. The important point is that a library that is contemplating buying or leasing a computer system should investigate the utility programs provided with the system, making certain that the proper utilities are provided for local library needs. The library will want to be sure that any utilities it requires (not included in the original system package) are available either separately from the manufacturer or from other vendors. There are many software vendors that specialize in writing commonly needed utilities for various computer manufacturers' systems.

One major difference between minicomputers and the larger computer systems is in this area of systems support software. Minicomputer manufacturers sell their systems for less; therefore, they cannot afford to create the extensive system support software that is available for mainframes.

SORT/MERGE UTILITIES

A sort utility program provides for the sorting of files on computer storage mediums. The following is a checklist of important questions about a sort utility program:

1. Will it sort in ascending order, descending order, or both?
2. Will it sort a file "in place," or does it require copying the file into sorted order on another storage area?
3. Does it sort in collating (character-code) sequence and/or numerical order?
4. How much extra work space does it require?
5. How fast is it?
6. Can it be invoked from an applications program or must it always be run by itself?
7. What storage mediums can it sort to and from?

Merge utilities take input files that have already been sorted on the same key and merge their contents into a single, larger file. Merge utilities represent either an option available in a comprehensive sort utility or a totally separate program. Most of the questions listed also are applicable to merge programs.

ACCESS METHODS

Access methods are system support programs used by applications programs to read and write records to and from files on storage mediums. Performance of I/O operations by access methods frees the programmer from concern over minute details of data handling, which are often particular to specific devices or manufacturers' methods. Access methods are usable by programs written in almost any programming language.

To facilitate this discussion of access methods, examples will be taken from IBM's software packages. Principles that are described will be generally applicable to software written by other vendors as well.

A major distinction among access methods is whether they are *basic*. A basic access method is less sophisticated, making it necessary for the applications programmer to do more work in a specific program. Using this kind of access method, a programmer must do the blocking and deblocking of records and buffering (these concepts were described in Chapter 3). Basic access methods also require the programmer to be responsible for I/O synchronization. Examples of basic access methods include the Basic Sequential Access Method (BSAM) and the Basic Direct Access Method (BDAM).

Higher level access methods aid the programmer in those areas mentioned. The Queued Sequential Access Method (QSAM), Indexed Sequential Access Method (ISAM), and Virtual Storage Access Method (VSAM) are representative of the more sophisticated access methods.

Input/output can also be done on a more primitive level than with basic access methods on computer systems. Such low-level data manipulation requires a great deal of programmer effort and knowledge. Given a choice, programmers always use the higher level access methods because of their convenience. About the only time basic or lower level input/output is used is when programmers wish to write the data input/output in some special manner perhaps not allowed in the higher level access methods. For instance, certain forms of BDAM may provide the quickest direct access available on a computer system. Systems programmers creating a real-time circulation control system might want to use BDAM because of its speed. BDAM's special property—direct access speed—might justify its use instead of VSAM, which is more convenient. The general rule when choosing among the relative levels of access methods is: the higher and more sophisticated, the better. Most programs, and almost all applications programs, use the highest level access method available for the system. The exceptions to this rule apply to special needs or situations, as in the example given.

The other distinguishing characteristic among access methods is the type(s) of access allowed. As can be seen from the names for which these acronyms stand, BSAM and QSAM offer sequential access only, while BDAM is for direct access only. Thus, a program that uses BSAM or QSAM to read and write data to and from a disk views the file on that disk as a sequential dataset. A program using BDAM for disk I/O considers the disk solely as a direct access device. Since tape cannot function as a directly accessed storage medium, BDAM may not be used in accessing tape files.

ISAM and VSAM are the most advanced of the higher level access methods, providing for either sequential or direct access as desired by the program using them. VSAM is IBM's latest generally used access method. It is more sophisticated than ISAM, in that it is capable of keeping files organized efficiently for its purposes, even after considerable updating has been done on the files. Under VSAM, a file can be expanded into more space as it is needed. With ISAM, files were much more static and tended to deteriorate after heavy file activity. ISAM files needed to be reloaded (i.e., ·performed by a utility program for this purpose) in order to remain efficient for processing. In general, ISAM is more versatile in the types of access it permits to files than are the basic and queued access methods. But VSAM, which is intended as a replacement for ISAM, offers ISAM's types of access with greater efficiency and sophistication.

Evaluation of access methods for versatility is similar to that concerning the relative levels of access methods. The library definitely wants a versatile access method offering different types of access to files, such as VSAM, or at least one that is equivalent to ISAM. More restrictive or specialized access methods would be needed only for special purposes or projects.

TEXT EDITORS

A *text editor* is a program that can be used via a terminal to enter data into the computer's files. This is the key-to-disk data entry referred to in Chapter 2.

Text editor programs operate in two basic modes. In the *data-entry mode*, the user of the text editor enters data line-by-line for storage in the computer. As each line is typed, it is displayed on the CRT screen or on the printing terminal paper so that it can be checked visually.

In the *command mode*, the user can give the text editor specific commands to list or alter files. If the user notices a misspelled word, forgets to enter a line, decides to insert a word, or wants to change punctuation, the text editor can be directed to make necessary alterations to the text through proper commands that it is given when in the command mode. Text editors always have a convenient method for switching between the data-entry and command modes. In many systems, for example, the user presses a special key or combination of keys to switch modes of operation.

Text editors are extremely useful support software for a number of reasons. They can be used for fast and accurate data entry into computer storage files in machine-readable form. An error made on a computer card means that the card must be discarded and another one keypunched, whereas on-line data entry with a text editor provides specific facilities for error correction. Thus, text editors enhance both the speed and accuracy of data entry. They can also be used to enter programs into computer files. Of course, any program must be entered into the system as data before it can be run.

Text editors can be evaluated on two main grounds. The first and most important is ease of use: Some text editors are easier to use because their commands are simpler to understand and remember. The second is range of function: Some text editors provide a wider and richer range of commands. Altogether, a text editor program represents an important systems support program at many library installations.

TELEPROCESSING

Implicit in the discussion on text editors is the assumption that many users could be *on-line* at the same time. An on-line system is one in which I/O devices, such as CRTs or other terminals, have access to machine-readable files through the computer.

Teleprocessing is the transmission of data over telephone and telegraph lines for remote terminal processing. The phrase "teleprocessing systems" often is used interchangeably with the term "on-line systems," although it is not strictly equivalent.

Some operating systems programs are more on-line and/or teleprocessing oriented than are others. For example, many minicomputer systems are sold for use as small on-line systems supporting 5 or 10 CRTs. The characters of on-line or teleprocessing operating systems can be quite different from those that are oriented primarily towards running batch-mode programs; for example, extra and/or different access methods may be used. IBM offers a Basic Telecommunications Access Method (BTAM), a Telecommunications Access Method (TCAM), and a Virtual Telecommunications Access Method (VTAM). The general orientation of an operating system in terms of teleprocessing should be researched and understood by interested librarians or analysts.

MULTIPROCESSING

Thus far, it has been implicitly assumed that any computing system has a single CPU. *Multiprocessing* refers to a computing system having more than one central processor. In a multiprocessing operating system, significant problems arise concerning the synchronization of and communications between the two (or more) CPUs.

Three basic approaches have been developed in response to these problems that are inherent in multiprocessing. In *loosely coupled multiprocessing* systems, jobs submitted to the system are assigned to a particular processor as they arrive, and that processor is then responsible for running the job. Variations of this approach are referred to as *coordinated job scheduling* or *separate systems*.

In a *master-slave* or *tightly coupled system,* one CPU is in charge of coordinating all processing within the system. The primary processor directs all processing, assigning discrete units of work to slave processors. The slave CPUs report back to the master processor as required tasks are completed.

A multiprocessing system that assumes equality among processors is the most difficult to implement. Operating systems permitting communication and coordination among these processors will be quite complex.

In all cases, the problems of coordinating processors involve software and processor overhead. As a computing system gets more CPUs, an ever-increasing amount of CPU efforts must be devoted to the overhead expense of synchronizing and coordinating the actions of the system.

SUMMARY

Kinds of systems support software that are available for most computing systems have been discussed in this chaper. Minicomputers, for instance, typically offer a smaller range of systems support software, since minicomputer manufacturers cannot afford to provide the kinds of software support offered for mainframes. Library analysts must be able to discern what systems software lacks in function versus when its spareness represents simplicity without any lesser quality or capacity. Subscribing to computer-user trade journals is the best way to develop this discriminatory ability and to keep pace with the rapid changes in software technology.

Other important aspects of systems support software are programming languages and their characteristics, since library programming requirements differ from those of industrial computer users. An introduction to programming languages is provided in the next chapter.

CHAPTER 8

Programming Languages

One of the most important aspects of systems software support is the programming languages available in the computing system. Various computer systems offer differing combinations of programming languages. Because libraries have specific and rather unusual software needs, the programming language(s) a computer system offers is especially important.

This chapter is intended to introduce the major software concepts concerning programming languages. These concepts are then analyzed and applied more specifically, in an evaluation of the programming needs of libraries and information centers.

MACHINE LANGUAGE

The hardware discussion in Chapter 1 explains the origins and purposes of programming languages. There, it was emphasized that the CPU is capable of interpreting and executing a given group of instructions. These instructions are referred to as its *instruction set*. Instruction sets for most processors range from a few dozen recognized instructions to several hundred instructions. Each one commands the CPU to perform one simple action. Instructions for any

NOTE: Portions of this chapter appeared in slightly modified form in the January 1979 issue of *Illinois Libraries*.

processor can be grouped into one of the few *instruction formats* used for that processor. A sample instruction is:

47FE

In this example, the "47" is the *operation code,* which tells the processor what operation to perform. The letters "F" and "E" are *operands,* or references to what to do the desired operation on. If one compares this message for the CPU to English, the operation code is the verb. It tells the CPU what to do. The operands are nouns that indicate what the action is to take place with or upon (Figure 42 illustrates this situation). Different instruction formats are relatively similar in structure to this example. Differences might be in the number of character positions reserved for the parts of the instruction, or in the number of operands the instruction has.

The instructions that a CPU can perform (i.e., those of its instruction set) are determined by the physical hardware of the central processor. Since they are related to the computer's architecture, they cannot be altered or changed for a computer once it is built. In addition, computers designed by different manufacturers, and

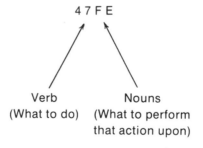

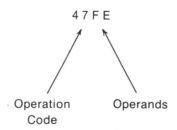

Figure 42   A MACHINE-LANGUAGE INSTRUCTION FORMAT.

even different models by the same manufacturer, do not have similar instruction sets. The instructions any given central processor can execute are called the *machine language, machine code,* or *object code* of that CPU.

The sample instruction of Figure 42 is typical of how machine language looks. An instruction is a string of contiguous characters, most of which are digits. A computer program written in machine language would consist of a large group of instructions similar to that shown in the example.

Since computers execute the machine-language instructions of their instruction set, the early programmers of the 1950s had to write programs in machine language. It was quickly discovered that this had numerous drawbacks, since programmers could not remember all of the various numbers and characters involved in the instructions. It was easy to make errors and very difficult to read a program. Underlying these problems was the simple fact that, although computers have to work in machine languages, it is complex, time-consuming, and tedious for programmers to try to work in these languages.

The resolution to this inherent man/machine conflict was both simple and brilliant. Why not write a machine-language program that could translate from a person-oriented language to the machine language? Then, a programmer could write a program in a familiar language and run the *language translator program* using that program as input data. The language translator program converts the programmer's submitted program into the equivalent machine-language instructions for the CPU to execute. After translation, the operating system runs the object code form of the programmer's submitted program. This process is diagrammed in Figure 43.

In the illustration, the language translator is kept resident on disk and is loaded into core and executed as necessary by the operating system. As explained in Chapter 5, the operating system receives details needed to do this correctly from the job control language (JCL) statements submitted to the system with the user job. The JCL, for instance, would tell the operating system which language translator program to use, such as FORTRAN, COBOL, or PL/1, if the system has more than one.

The first language translator programs written were called

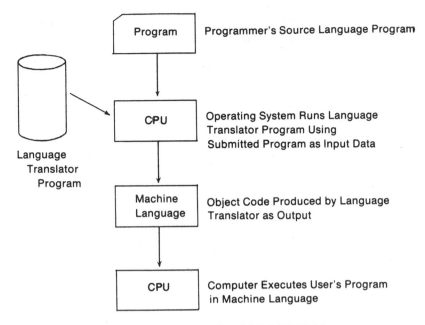

Figure 43 THE LANGUAGE TRANSLATOR PROCESS.

assemblers or *assembly language*. These assembly translator programs offered several advantages to writing programs in machine languages. First, *mnemonic abbreviations* were used for individual instructions instead of the numeric operation codes of machine language. In Figure 42, for example, the operation code was "47." An assembly language would allow a programmer to write a mnemonic abbreviation of "BC" for this operation. Similarly, in machine language, an addition operation could be a "5A." An assembly language might allow "A" or even "ADD" to indicate this operation. Thus, assembly languages are more human oriented than machine languages, although assembler mnemonics are still rather cryptic.

Assembly languages also allow more flexibility and clarity in programming when programmers must reference specific locations within computer memory in their programs. For example, in order to reference a place in main memory in machine language, the programmer is required to use a number representing that position, such as "00089902." Assembly languages provide a mechanism for programmers to name that location in memory. "00089902" might always be referred to by the word "VARIABLE," for example, whenever a reference to that location in memory must be made. Again, the rules for naming locations in memory in assembly languages are rather strict. Still, it should be clear to the reader that using short words and abbreviations in programming is easier than using machine-language numbers.

The defining or distinguishing characteristic of assembly languages is that each assembly-language instruction translates into one machine-language instruction. Thus, assemblers are fairly close to machine languages in this critical regard.

Most assembly languages do provide *macro instructions* or *macros* that translate into a multiplicity of machine-language instructions. These can aid in separating the programmer from the level of detail involved in programming where each assembler instruction corresponds to one machine-language instruction. Macro instructions, however, account for a minority of the instructions in most assembly-language programs. In general, assembly languages can be characterized as being composed of instructions that translate on a one-to-one basis into corresponding machine-language instructions.

Languages that are more human oriented than the assembly languages were developed in the late 1950s and early 1960s. These programs are called *compilers*. Compilers are language translators with their own syntactical and linguistic rules that allow a *source program* written in the language to be translated into object code.

Compiler instructions typically convert to a group of machine instructions. Thus, it is easier for programmers to write in these higher level languages than in assembly language. Since compilers are higher level translators, they switch the burden of man/machine communication to the computer itself. This means that programmer productivity is higher when compilers are used. It also implies that maintenance tasks are easier. The disadvantage is that the programmer is at a distance from the true operations and capabilities of the computer; that is, the programmer is more dependent on the characteristics of the compiler. The choice of programming language may, therefore, affect the ease of solving a programming problem. When the programming-language characteristics coincide with the nature of the programming problem, an easy resolution of the problem can be achieved. Otherwise, difficulties may be encountered.

The third type of language translator is the *interpreter*, which will be discussed later in this chapter.

Notice that with both assembly and the higher level languages, programmers follow a two-step process in testing or *debugging* their programs. First, they run their programs in order to eliminate the syntactical errors. Only then will the program be intelligible to the language translator. The submitted program will be executed by the central processor only if it has been translated by the language translator without error. Thus, in the translation phase of their programs' debugging, programmers deal with linguistic and syntactical errors. In the actual execution phase of testing, programmers must correct logical or processing errors.

The first phase of program debugging requires knowledge of the linguistic rules of the language translator being used and is aided by language manual documentation. The second phase, the correcting of logical errors, involves the use of such logical tools as *program flowcharts, decision tables, pseudocode,* or *Warnier diagrams.* The topical index of this book's bibliography refers to these tools of logical design under the subject heading of ''Systems Analysis and Design.''

LIBRARY PROGRAMMING

Most sources in library and information science approach the topic of programming languages with language-by-language characterization and analysis of each of the major languages in relation to library applications. This section will present a different approach. The types of programming problems and situations most likely to arise in library and information center programming will be analyzed, and the suitability and capabilities of particular programming languages will be discussed within this context. The programming requirements of many library tasks are very similar to those found in business, industrial, and governmental programming environments. Libraries, however, have numerous programming applications peculiar to their own institutional purposes, including such applications as keyword indexing, document retrieval, selective dissemination of information (SDI) and current awareness functions, and the production of bibliographies, abstracts, and other textual documents.

Systems Programming

First, it is appropriate to discuss library programming situations that are similar to those encountered in other organizations using computers. The commonly accepted distinction between data processing and systems programming is useful here. Data-processing applications involve using the computer to speedily dispatch large amounts of clerical work of a highly repetitive nature. Systems programming refers to support and maintenance of the kinds of system support software discussed in Chapter 7. This would include any programming time spent in installing, modifying, or enhancing the operating system itself.

It is clear that systems programming within the specific context of the library or information center environment will be necessary for the support, maintenance, and enhancement of systems software. For example, installation of a database system, similar to those discussed in Chapter 10, would entail systems programming.

The creation and maintenance of certain internal programs to support functional library systems or subsystems also might involve systems programming. Examples could include programs to create an on-line "card catalog" system, implementation programs for an on-line circulation system, and programs for a serials check-in system via computer terminal entry.

In industrial situations, systems programming is usually synonymous with the use of lower level assembly languages. Assembly languages, sometimes referred to as "assembler" or by the name for a particular assembly language, such as BAL or Autocoder, may be contrasted with the procedure-oriented or compiler-level languages of much wider recognition (e.g., FORTRAN,

COBOL, PL/1, and others), in that assembler is much closer to machine language. The assembly languages are characterized by the one-to-one correspondence of their instructions to those of machine languages. Thus, assembler languages yield much greater power and control to the programmer in such areas as addressability, bit manipulation, and storage allocation, among others. This is the basis for using the more complex and difficult assembly languages—systems programming often requires this level of specificity in its programming capabilities.

All kinds of computer users, including libraries, often have been more or less required to use the lower level languages to implement all or particular parts of systems programs. Once written and tested, such a systems program is converted to object (machine) code and kept resident on disk for faster access and run time, since the program does not need to be reassembled. A systems program implies constant use of the code once generated, and, thus, a single conversion to object code is most efficient.

If libraries require a certain amount of systems programming that often cannot be accomplished through the use of higher level languages, what are the implications of using assembly languages with which librarians, library analysts and systems designers, information scientists, and administrators should be familiar?

The lower level languages are complex. Unless information center personnel are advanced computer specialists, they cannot be expected to deal with these languages. Although a library using COBOL or PL/1 might employ its own information scientists or librarians with some programming knowledge, in order to use assembly languages, there is no alternative to the need for computer programmers and specialists. Programmers who write assembly code generally are more highly trained, higher paid personnel than those who work in applications programming in the higher level languages. Thus, library expense for programmers to write and maintain programs in the lower level languages is higher than for other languages, due to the length and complexity involved in such programming.

Assembly-language programming is less likely to be well documented, or to use such techniques as structured flowcharting. This also limits the intelligibility of such programming to library and administrative personnel.

Most important, assembly languages are not machine independent. Different manufacturers, and even different machines by the same manufacturer, will use different assembly languages. All IBM 360s, for example, use the same assembly language, but this code would definitely not be transferable to Honeywell or Burroughs machines. This factor has distinct implications for the sharing or cooperative use of programs among libraries where systems programming or assembly languages may be involved.

Since assembly language is closer to machine language, more efficient programs may be produced; such programs may cost substantially less for each run. When a program is run either many times daily or continuously, as in the examples of on-line library systems mentioned earlier, savings in execution time costs may be significant. This can counterbalance initially higher costs in creating and maintaining assembly programs.

Obviously, these languages are the province of computer programmers only. They will not be understood by information scientists and librarians unless they have or acquire specific knowledge of this type of programming. But, unavoidably, a certain portion of systems programming must be written in assembly language, so the internal aspects of many library systems may be implemented with a lower level language. Therefore, knowledge of the implications of assembly usage may prove highly useful to librarians, administrators, and information scientists. Further background discussion and applications of the lower level languages can be found in the bibliography at the end of this book.

Data Processing

A second major area of programming common to libraries, information centers, and other organizations using computers is *data processing*. Data processing is the use of computers to perform repetitive clerical tasks. Similar to businesses, libraries may use computers in payroll applications, accounting systems, and for inventory functions. A classic example of the similarity between library and other data-processing systems may be found in the batch-mode circulation systems that were popular in the 1960s;

these were the common data-processing systems of file maintenance for input editing, updating, utility sorts, and report generation.

The language of business data processing is overwhelmingly COmmon Business Oriented Language (COBOL). Designed specifically for the tasks of business data processing, COBOL enjoys wide computer support and use and is familiar to the majority of professional programmers and many others. In this context, it should be remembered that a major factor in selecting the software for an institution with limited financial support should be the availability of the language as well as its suitability.

Due to these considerations, COBOL does have widespread use in libraries. But COBOL has a specific disadvantage for library use in that it is not amenable to the third major area of library programming applications to be discussed in this chapter.

Programming Language/One (PL/1) also is a highly suitable language for the data-processing needs of the library. Like COBOL, it features all of the advantages of the major higher level languages: machine independence, a standard compiler and documentation standard, great power with less complexity than the lower level languages, and an opportunity for information science professionals to do their own programming rather than rely on outside specialists or computer professionals.

In relation to the data-processing needs of libraries, then, both COBOL and PL/1 are highly suitable languages. Both have specific advantages and liabilities that will be enumerated in more detail later in this discussion.

Unique Library Processing Needs

The third major area of library programming needs consists of programs whose logic would be found only in libraries or information centers, due to the institutional purposes of these organizations. Much of this processing would be concerned with the manipulation of bibliographic records, for example, to print bibliographies or documents listings for SDI or current awareness needs. Other examples would include KWIC and KWOC indexes, serials listings, topical listings of various sorts, concordances, and glossaries. Nonsystems programming for information retrieval (IR) also would fall into this category.

Thus, there are a number of programs whose logic and needs are peculiar to libraries and information centers. Note that the outstanding characteristic of these library-type programs is that information is nonnumeric or noncomputational. As was discussed in Chapter 1, this sort of information is best stored in a character format. This fact leads directly to the programming requirements involved—string-processing facilities are needed in the software selected.

Basically, a *string* may be defined as a group of symbols selected from a character set having some meaningful internal order and a finite length. A *character string* is merely a string of characters, digits, special characters, and blanks immediately adjacent to one another, with an implied length. A primary characteristic of strings and their manipulation is the uncertainty or unpredictability governing their lengths. Variable-length fields and records are the rule here. This contrasts to their status in data processing as an exception one would hope to avoid.

The preeminent examples of strings in common library programming are book and journal titles. A given title is usually under 100 characters in length, but it could be longer. The title normally would consist of letters and spaces, or it could contain other characters. Punctuation marks and digits are frequently encountered nonalphabetic characters. Book and journal titles epitomize many of the problems and requirements of string handling in information-center programming.

In relation to the nonsystems and non-data-processing needs of libraries, then, software must be capable of character-string manipulation. The language must be able to combine or *concatenate* strings, *bifurcate* or separate strings into substring fields, and determine equality or inequality between strings and substrings.

Two languages are particularly noted for their string-manipulation facility—StriNg Oriented symBOlic Language (SNOBOL) and COMIT. Their current versions are referred to as SNOBOL4 and COMIT II.

SNOBOL4 is the more widespread of the two languages. Developed at Bell Telephone Laboratories, the language is oriented toward string-processing procedures such as matching substrings and bifurcation. But the price of this capability in string and variable-length field operations is a language not suited to general usage. SNOBOL4 might be used only with difficulty, for example, in the general data-processing functions of the library, because its arithmetic and editing (printing) capabilities are somewhat limited.

A part of SNOBOL's power in relation to variable-length fields is the fact that it runs as an *interpreter* rather than as a compiler. Program statements may be interpreted at the time of execution, rather than converted to object code prior to execution by a multipass assembler process. The advantage is that storage may be dynamically allocated at the time of execution, for better accommodation of variable-length records or strings. But the drawback is that even serially reusable programs cannot be kept on disk in object code. A program must be reinterpreted each time it is run, and turnaround is very slow for an interpreter.

SNOBOL4 has been reworked into a true compiler in the form of SPeedy ImplemenTation of SNOBOL (SPITBOL). SPITBOL runs faster than the interpreter version and produces object code; however, distribution of the SPITBOL compiler is still fairly limited.

Another compiler version of SNOBOL is SNOBAT. Similar to SPITBOL, this compiler runs faster than the SNOBOL interpreter, and it requires less main memory for execution. But, like SPITBOL, SNOBAT suffers from limited availability.

Similarly, COMIT was designed specifically in relation to string-processing capabilities. As a very high-level language, it is relatively simple to learn, yielding great string-processing power to even the minimally trained. Furthermore, it has been successfully applied to information retrieval applications as well. Even though SNOBOL4 is a recognizable name to most computer professionals, COMIT has always remained in the experimental realm; it is strictly a special-purpose language having very little in the way of arithmetic operators. Thus, COMIT often has proved useful in relation to specific information storage and retrieval (ISR) and information retrieval (IR) projects and experiments, but it is difficult to visualize it in the role of widespread or general library usage.

The two principal string-manipulation languages now have been discussed briefly. Description has been kept minimal, due to previous coverage of the potential of these languages in other papers for the information scientist. Further information on these languages can be located through this book's bibliography.

In relation to specifically library-oriented programming, PL/I presents some useful features. This is the only general-purpose language designed with character-string capabilities. PL/I has a concatenation operator and functions for substrings, index, length, translating, and verifying. Thus, PL/I not only can be used very easily for the data-processing operations of the library but also has string-manipulating facilities not found in COBOL. Furthermore, PL/I can be implemented in an interactive mode, and learning variants of the compiler are available, such as PL/C, QI-PL/I, and SP/k. Several subsets have been implemented on minicomputers. Microcomputer versions called PL/M and PL/I-80 also are available.

COBOL offers no specific instructions for character-string operations (exceptions in IBM's Version 4 compiler are EXAMINE/INSPECT, STRING, UNSTRING, and TRANSFORM), but the language can be used with variable-length records. H. Avram and J. R. Droz[1] describe COBOL usage with variable-length fields and variable-length records in the case of MARC II at the Library of Congress. The verdict on COBOL for this particular library application, then, must be that it can be used with variable-length records. But PL/I definitely offers better potential for string-processing situations, with its more sophisticated instructions included in the compiler specifically for this purpose.

In reference to character-string manipulation, other major languages are similar to COBOL. They have some minor capabilities through extensions of the languages rather than by design. FORTRAN (FORmula TRANslator) can be used in certain situations, the WATFIV (WATerloo version of FORTRAN IV) compiler providing the fullest version of the language for these purposes. ALGOL has similar extensions.

Thus, PL/I is the only general-purpose language with strong string-manipulation capability. SNOBOL4 is a highly developed,

[1]H. Avram and J. R. Droz. "MARC II and COBOL." *Journal of Library Automation,* *1*(4):261–272, December 1968.

special-purpose, string-processing language of fairly wide implementation. The SPITBOL and SNOBAT variants of SNOBOL and COMIT II are infrequently encountered compilers of strong capability in this area. COMIT, particularly, is specialized in its orientation. Other major high-level languages could be used for string-manipulation and/or information retrieval programming, but most of these have only limited facilities included through extensions. Their use could necessitate extensive subroutine writing for particular string-processing needs.

Operations Research

A final area to consider in library programming is operations research. Examples here include simulation techniques and computer circulation studies. Software requirements would be determined by the nature of the individual application. As mentioned previously, COMIT could prove useful in information retrieval experiments. Lower level languages might be required for certain other applications. Mathematical languages, such as FORTRAN, APL (A Programming Language), or BASIC (Beginners All-purpose Symbolic Instruction Code), might find their major application to library and information science in operations research. Again, general-purpose PL/1 can be used for mathematical programming.

SUMMARY

Library and information-center software requirements are similar to those encountered in business and other organizations in the areas of systems programming and data processing. But libraries do have programming needs peculiar to their own institutional purposes. Character-format data, string manipulation, and complementary data structures distinguish the programming requirements peculiar to the information-handling techniques common in libraries.

In systems programming, lower level assembly languages may be required for some programming because of the greater specificity and power they give to programmers. Also, these languages generally yield more efficient programs. In situations where assembly routines are run many times daily, the cost savings can successfully outweigh the initial higher cost involved in creating and maintaining such programs. Assembly programs, however, are machine-dependent. Due to the many implications for system design resulting from the differences between the assembly and compiler-level languages, persons involved in administration, systems analysis, and many other areas of library and information science should be familiar with these considerations.

To meet the software needs of library data processing, both COBOL and PL/1 are widely available and capable languages. PL/1, however, presents a number of advantages for more general library use. This language is highly versatile and especially useful for mathematically oriented programming such as simulation and operations research. At the same time, it is a general-purpose language designed with capability for string manipulation and processing of character-format data.

Other features of PL/1 include its modularity, the availability of many structured texts for the language, the texts designed specifically for librarians and information scientists, and the relative ease of learning the language. To elaborate further on the relative ease of learning PL/1, the language has a subset nature based on numerous default options, allowing the beginner to program successfully by using only those portions of the language that are familiar to him. Many of the language constructs, such as the DO loop, are implemented in a manner similar to FORTRAN. Furthermore, PL/1 has certain language features analogous to those encountered in COBOL.[2] Finally, the existence of learning and academic compilers for the language has been noted.

Because of PL/1's versatility and the other factors already mentioned, the consensus of the library community seems to be that PL/1 is the language of choice for general use. The PL/1 texts and the

[2]For a description of PL/1's similarities to FORTRAN and COBOL, see H. Fosdick, "Opting for PL/1: The Strengths of PL/1 Offset the Weaknesses of COBOL," *Computerworld*, *14*(32):27–30, August 11, 1980.

sources in the bibliography substantiate this conclusion. Also, a survey by this author indicates that PL/I is the most widely taught programming language in graduate library schools. [3]

In any given instance of software implementation, however, local factors may be paramount. For example, if a library were to be involved only in data-processing applications and not in programming for many distinctive "library" applications, the use of COBOL would prove quite adequate.

Also, data from a recent survey[4] shows that PL/I is a distant third in popularity for business data-processing applications (trailing COBOL and assembler). Junior colleges, for example, sometimes do not teach PL/I. The implication here is that libraries or information centers in a few localities might experience more difficulty in hiring PL/I programmers than in securing COBOL expertise. On the other hand, persons already on the library staff more likely would be experienced in PL/I rather than any other language. Experience suggests that availability of software selection is as important a concept as suitability.

To an important extent, of course, a discussion determining the single most capable programming language for library applications is academic—few computer users rely on a single language for all their programming needs. [4] Moreover, few computers, except some mini- and microcomputers, come equipped with only a single compiler. A library is most likely to have a few programming languages available for its use. Therefore, a combination of an assembly language, a data-processing or general-purpose compiler, and a string-manipulation language would be particularly desirable in a library programming environment. If resources to support such an idea combination are not available, the author hopes that this chapter has provided a framework for the conceptualization and analysis of library software considerations important in information-center programming situations.

[3]H. Fosdick. "Library Education in Information Science: Present Trends." *Special Libraries,* 69(3):100–108, May 1978.

[4]A. S. Philappakis. "A Popularity Contest for Languages." *Datamation,* 23(12):81–87, December 1977.

CHAPTER 9

Documentation

Documentation is an important, yet often neglected, aspect of library computer systems. Proper documentation describes all areas of the library's programming projects and software. The specific areas into which documentation requirements can be categorized are user, program, systems and project, and managerial.

In this chapter, these documentation categories are discussed to determine why documentation is so important in any computer system. The term "documentation" in computer systems refers to explanatory or descriptive documents created for computer software systems. These documents may be generated as part of a systems project, or they may be written in the course of the normal operation of an existing system. But the key point is that they should be written, because often they are not. When underdocumentation occurs, it represents a potentially disastrous managerial error in setting up a new system, or in establishing documentation procedures for an existing system. The wasted effort and loss of productivity that can result from inadequate documentation are astounding. Unfortunately, even though numerous examples exist of data-processing centers and libraries that have experienced problems because of insufficient documentation, many libraries do not understand proper documentation procedures or are reluctant to follow through on them. This natural tendency towards underdocumenting projects and systems will be explored in the sections that follow. First, examples of inadequate and adequate documentation are presented.

Figure 44 shows part of an assembly-language computer program that lacks adequate documentation. Compare this program with that of Figure 45, which displays a more adequate level of program documentation. In Figure 45, each individual instruction has English-language comments to the right of it, which serve to clarify and explain what the instructions on the left are supposed to be doing.

Furthermore, the program documentation in Figure 45 includes substantial commentary on the purposes and other crucial aspects of the program. The particular computer language of Figure 45 allows programmers to document their programs by placing an asterisk character at the beginning of any line. Then, whatever the programmer wishes to write in the remainder of the statement is treated solely as a comment by the computer-systems software. In other words, these comment statements are a facility provided in programming languages for the express purpose of allowing programmers to enter an explanation of their programs in English.

Without any knowledge of computer programming or programming languages, it should be easy to see that the program of Figure 45 is infinitely more valuable than that of Figure 44. If one remembers that maintenance programming—making modifications to existing programs—consumes most programmer time, which of these two programs would be easier to alter? Clearly, a programmer would spend more time simply trying to figure out what purposes and methodologies are used in the first program. Given the logical complexity of many programs, this would be no small task.

As a second example of the value of documentation, consider the illustration of Figure 45 again. Here is a well-documented, properly working program. Like most programs at typical installations, it will be stored on disk in both its original source language and object code forms. Is there adequate documentation elsewhere describing what this program is, what it does, when it is to be run, and where and how to retrieve it from disk storage? If not, this program may simply be lost.

For example, if there is no documentation providing the file name on which the copies of this program reside, no one will be able to find the program in the computer-systems storage. This is exactly analogous to shelving a new book without first cataloging it and placing information on it in the card catalog. A computing

```
* SEARCH RTN. BY H. FOSDICK
SEARCH    $BEGIN
          LM        R2,R4,0(R1)      GET PARMS
          ST        R2,PARMHASH
          LA        R1,PARMHASH
          $CALL     HASH             CALL HASH
          L         R6,HASHVAL
          SLA       R6,2
          AR        R6,R3            ADD VALUES

          L         R2,0(R2)
          USING     $BADF,R6
          L         R7,$LINKF
          USING     $BADC,R7
          LTR       R7,R7            IS CURRENT 0?
          BZ        ENDDO            GO
```

Figure 44   AN INADEQUATELY DOCUMENTED COMPUTER PROGRAM.

system without documentation is equivalent to a library organization without proper cataloging procedures. To expand upon these examples, there are four general purposes of documentation: to provide for accurate, precise communication through a more or less permanent medium; to provide historical information or data useful for future reference; to delimit and define exact performance criteria for projects or systems; and to provide self-instructional material on systems created by specialists to be used by a broad spectrum of users. All of these objectives are applicable to the four documentation categories, that is, user, program, systems and project, and managerial documentation. Each category will be discussed in detail.

USER DOCUMENTATION

User documentation is written by the creators of a system for those who will actually operate or use the system. The intended

```
:·····································································································
:NAME: SEARCH                                                    BY: H. FOSDICK
:
:FUNCTION: THE SEARCH ROUTINE CALLS THE 'HASH' SUBRTN. TO
:          HASH THE BINARY BOOK ID TO CALCULATE AN ENTRY
:          ADDRESS INTO THE HASH TABLE. SEARCH THEN SEARCHES
:          THE CHAIN STARTING AT THAT HASH TABLE ADDRESS FOR
:          THE KEY.
:
:INPUT: NONE                                                     OUTPUT: NONE
:
:ENTRY: R1 POINTS TO THE ADDRESSES OF:
:       BINARY BOOK ID
:       HASH TABLE
:       THE PLACE INTO WHICH TO PUT 'FORMER' (SEE 'DRIV.B')
:
:EXIT: FORMER RETURNED. RETURN CODE IN R15 AS FOLLOWS:
:
:                       0—KEY FOUND
:                       4—KEY NOT FOUND IN FILE
:
:REGISTERS USED: R13—BASE FOR THE CSECT
:                R6—BASE FOR $BADF DSECT
:                R7—BASE FOR $BADC DSECT
:
:·····································································································

        *
SEARCH  $BEGIN                          ENTER VIA STANDARD LINKAGE
        LM        R2,R4,0(R1)           LOAD PARAMETERS
        *                               R2—ADDRESS OF BINARY BK ID
        *                               R3—ADDRESS OF HASH TABLE
        *                               R4—ADDRESS OF FORMER POS.
        *
        ST        R2,PARMHASH           PASS BK ID TO 'HASH'
        LA        R1,PARMHASH           POINT R1 TO PARMLIST
        $CALL     HASH                  CALL HASH ROUTINE
        *
        *
        L         R6,HASHVAL            GET HASH VALUE INTO R6
        SLA       R6,2                  MULTIPLY IT BY 4
        AR        R6,R3                 ADD ADDRESS HASH TABLE TO IT
        *
        *
        L         R2,0(R2)              GET BK ID INTO R2
        USING     $BADF,R6              R6 BASE FOR $BADF DSECT
        L         R7,$LINKF             R7 IS NOW CURRENT
        USING     $BADC,R7              R7 BASE FOR $BADC DSECT
        LTR       R7,R7                 IS CURRENT 0?
        BZ        ENDDO                 YES, TO ENDDO
                  .         .
                  .         .
                  .         .
```

Figure 45   A WELL-DOCUMENTED COMPUTER PROGRAM.

users probably will be a broad and varied group of persons with profoundly differing abilities to understand the created system. The designers of the functional system usually will have a better comprehension of the technical aspects of the system's internal functioning than the users will have. System designers must remember, however, to communicate technical knowledge concerning the system only where it is of direct interest and importance to those using the system. Technological breakthroughs or other outstanding internal aspects of the system are just that—internal aspects. As such, they are of little relevance to persons who will operate or use the system. User documentation must describe what the users need and want to know, not what the system's designers prefer to document.

User documentation consists of two kinds of information: first, exact specification of user personnel procedures and methodologies, and, second, a more general explanation of how an individual user's actions complement the purposes and functions of the larger system. The first type of information ensures that the user can find complete and accurate coverage about what he might want to do with the system or might be confronted with by the system. The user can respond effectively to whatever situation is implicit vis-à-vis the system. The second type of information merely refers to the fact that the user should be given some appreciation of his role in the system as a whole. Leaving a user without a general understanding of the purposes of the system he is attempting to use can have negative consequences unforeseen by the system's designers.

To relate this discussion to specific library examples, the creators of library computer systems are those computer-systems personnel discussed in Chapter 2. Library systems analysts most likely would be the authors of the user documentation. The users of the system would be other library employees, depending on the system's purpose. The primary users of an on-line serials check-in system might be clerical staff, although librarians as well would want to know how to use the system. Circulation control systems also are used primarily by clerical staff, librarians again needing to understand the system's operation. Cataloging-aid systems would have professional librarians as their users, and on-line catalogs might have totally "untutored" patrons in the user group; thus, the library's functional programming systems may have a wide range of users. The important point is that library systems analysts, or whoever is responsible for user documentation, explicitly recognize who the users are.

Once the user groups have been defined and recognized, documentation can be written and explicitly directed toward their needs. Documentation should not make unwarranted assumptions concerning the relative sophistication of users. Documentation for an on-line catalog query system, for instance, should not assume knowledge of the library or library terms if library patrons will be using the system. On the other hand, this documentation may assume such knowledge if use of the system is restricted to professional librarians. In this case, the writers of user documentation must not include technical computer terms without explanation. In each case, documentation must be designed for and relevant to the ablities and characteristics of its users. The documentation must be all-inclusive in its coverage of possible interactions of users with the system. It should relate this specific view of the system to the purposes and functions of the system as a whole.

PROGRAM DOCUMENTATION

This category of documentation refers to all of the documentation necessary for the writing, maintenance, and running of computer programs. Program documentation can be divided into documentation actually contained within the program and documentation relevant to the program but existing elsewhere.

Figure 45 has been provided to give an example of a fully documented routine. A *routine* is a logical subportion of a computer program. For each routine encoded, some statement of name, function (or purpose), inputs and outputs, entry and exit conditions to the routine, and programming notes should be written. All programming languages have facilities allowing for such documentation in the programs. *These should be used.* Differing languages also have various indentation rules and other method-ologies for making them easier to read and follow. Higher level languages, discussed in Chapter 8, offer some additional "self-documenting" capabilities. In comparative studies, programs written in higher level languages have proved to be easier to maintain than their assembly-language counterparts.[1]

Program documentation not stored in machine-readable form with the program usually is kept in a program documentation folder. One folder is maintained for each program at the installation. The minimum material that each folder should contain is:

1. General information on the program, equivalent to that just discussed and found in the program.

2. Input-data documents and specifications and output report format(s) and specifications. File names, descriptions, and record layouts should be included.

3. Statements of program methodology and logic that might be expressed in formats or forms such as flowcharts, decision tables, Warnier diagrams, pseudocode, block diagrams, and other forms of logical expression.

4. A copy of the original program specification, if it is distinct from points 1, 2, and 3. In many shops, this documentation folder will be the only form of program specification.

There are other places where program documentation will exist in the system for particular purposes, other than in the documentation folder and the program. Most installations keep a programming *Standards and Conventions Handbook,* which may be only an informal collection of commentary outlining general programming requirements; for instance, the handbook would give programmers a guide to program-interfacing standards.

There also must be program documentation so operations personnel can answer questions on what data files need to be set up

---

[1] See, for example, the following:

F. P. Brooks. *The Mythical Man-Month.* Reading, Mass., Addison-Wesley, 1975, pp. 88–94.

V. Schneider. "Prediction of Software and Project Duration: Four New Formulas." *SIGPLAN Notices, 13* (6):49–59, June 1978.

in order to run a program, when and how the program should be run, and what should be done in the event of certain error messages. For large or long-running programs, some sort of *error restart* procedure should be specified. This avoids rerunning a program if it should fail during processing. Operations personnel usually have a *run book* that keeps this kind of program information available.

Finally, there is documentation pertaining to how an individual program fits into a programming system. In this discussion, such documentation is treated in the section that follows: Project and Systems Documentation.

Program documentation, as important as it is, is either totally inadequate or simply not written at many computer installations. This observation pertains to both business and library computer users. Given the possibly dire consequences of poor documentation, why is this form of documentation so often neglected?

Programmers are responsible for program documentation within a program, but in most programming situations, documentation is not measured in the evaluations made of programmer productivity. Programmers are typically under pressure to do "more important" things, and some simply dislike documenting. Systems analysts are subject to similar pressures. Documentation folders may consist of no more than original notes on program specifications. As maintenance is performed on the program, these folders quickly become outdated and misleading unless they reflect the changes made in the program.

Bias against program documentation is rampant at many computer installations, and libraries are no exception. Unfortunately, the consequences of poor program documentation can be severe. One consequence has already been pointed out—the loss of programmer time through making maintenance tasks many times more difficult than they have to be. The natural tendency to "cut corners" by omitting documentation during the original writing of a program is paid for many times over by time wasted during program maintenance—maintenance is the most time-intensive form of programmer activity.

Another consequence of neglecting program documentation is

the need for a total rewrite of programs. It is sometimes easier for a programmer to start fresh than to attempt to decode tricky or obscure undocumented programming. Horror stories of the scrapping of entire programming systems are true, although rare. A massively expensive effort involved in understanding un-documented systems is usually attempted, often followed by a difficult retroactive documentation task.

The high degree of computing personnel mobility aggravates the problems associated with undocumented programming. When a programmer leaves a firm, any programs he was respon-sible for now become maintenance headaches unless they are properly documented. The same is true of any programming systems with which the programmer was familiar. Relying on one person's knowledge of programs or systems can be the most grievous error that computing systems management can commit. Accidents and changes in employee health must be considered, as well as employee turnover. No computer-system employee should be indispensable to the effective operation or the continuance of either functional systems or individual programs. In the library, as elsewhere, good documentation is the best insurance the in-stallation can have against such loss-of-knowledge situations.

Program documentation also lends information a permanency over time that cannot be achieved through human memory, even when no personnel changes occur. How many library program-mers can recall specific characteristics of a little-used program written two years earlier? Program documentation is essential in its role of providing historical data for future reference.

One argument against spending time on program documenta-tion is that programming systems are so subject to change that this investment of time in documenting soon-to-be obsolete soft-ware is not worthwhile. This view overlooks the phenomenon of continuity between systems. When a new system is to be de-signed, creation will not occur in a vacuum. Certain features will be based on or developed from details of the previous system. Im-provements and modifications of the previous system can be achieved only with the sort of historical perspective gained through the documentation associated with that system. To put it another way, even the certainty of software obsolescence argues in favor of adequate documentation in order to learn from past mistakes and to improve software performance.

In conclusion, libraries tend to follow the established industrial pattern of slighting program documentation, which may be due to the small size of library programming staff. This shortsighted saving of effort usually leads directly to lower quality systems, which create greater expenditures in the long run. Time spent on documentation is truly "invested," in that it will yield returns.

In a small data-processing department, programming standards and documentation usually are treated informally—there will be no programmer's guide to standards. In this situation, programmers will most likely allow documentation to lapse as a low-priority task. Program documentation has been emphasized, because this author strongly feels that this is the one area of documentation in which libraries trail behind the modern practices of the leading industrial computer installations.

PROJECT AND SYSTEMS DOCUMENTATION

A *programming system* is a group of programs written to achieve a single larger purpose. *Systems documentation* refers to the documentation resulting from the need to describe and explain programming systems. As systems documentation develops from or is a product of a programming project, the documents produced over the lifetime of programming projects should be produced in stages.

A *feasibility study* is a document resulting from first considerations of the problem to be solved by a programming system. Much of it is based on the definition of the problem and estimates of the resources required to accomplish a solution. Time, cost, and the resulting system's quality all are covered in the feasibility study.

In the early definition phase of a project, a *project plan* may be written. This document outlines a plan for conducting the project. It provides documentation defining the problem and how the project to solve it will be organized and carried out. The project plan consists of detailed descriptions of particular aspects of the project, including personnel, equipment resources, testing, and installation plans.

The *problem specification* document contains a definition of the problem and the performance criteria that a solution system is designed to meet. This document would be complemented by a design specification that details the solution actually chosen for implementation. The *design specification* describes the solution to the problem and contains explicit data on the expected performance of this solution relevant to those criteria outlined in the problem specification.

Although these documents obviously would be subject to change during the life of the project, separate documentation often is kept to record changes to the original design solution during the project. A *project history* folder or a *project personnel handbook* is used for this purpose.

Of the suggested documents for project and systems documentation, most will be used in some combination at computer installations engaged in important projects. Libraries should be no exception. The natural tendency to do things informally, which is evident on smaller projects or in smaller library computer shops, should definitely be avoided. Written specifications and decisions are essential to the coherence, conceptual integrity, and direction required in any successful project. The most frequently underestimated and underrated aspect of any computer project is the vital importance of planning. Project and systems documentation will go a long way toward forcing adequate project planning; upon the project's completion, this documentation provides a broad base for any remaining systems documentation to be written.

Thus, project documentation may be necessary both during the project and as systems documentation results upon conclusion of the project. Needless to say, documentation is invariably required for justification and analysis of any library programming project to library management. Commitment to thoroughness at the project's start can fulfill this purpose as well as project and systems documentation needs.

MANAGERIAL DOCUMENTATION

As previously stated, the library administration will want its own documentation on the library's programming systems. This documentation need is distinct from those categories of documentation previously discussed. Library management will require documentation to get an overall view of the purposes and goals of library programming systems. Basic requirements and methods relating to the achievement of system functions should be delineated, whether the system is new or already in use.

For new systems, library administration will need documentation to monitor progress made as the system develops. Documents that satisfy this information requirement have been mentioned in the section on Project and Systems Documentation.

For currently operational systems, library administration will need documentation that reflects performance criteria and how the system is functioning in relation to these criteria. Documentation can serve to aid management in its evaluations of systems operation, as well as in its quest for system improvement.

SUMMARY

In this chapter, the purposes of documentation and the kinds of documentation found in computing systems in general have been discussed. As the importance of documentation is not appreciated by many computer users, reasons for proper and full documentation have been explained.

Libraries that have reasonable documentation in relation to user, management, and project and system needs will commonly ignore the need for good program documentation. Unfortunately, problems in the programs of library automation projects are found at least as often as elsewhere in such systems. Given the realities of maintenance programming, the wisest course is to be prepared for the inevitable by adequate program documentation. Library administrators should be aware of the latest program documentation practices and should require their computer staff to adhere to standards reflecting these practices. To assist the reader, sources on the topic are provided in the annotated bibliography.

CHAPTER 10

Database Systems

When librarians hear the phrase "database systems," the major computerized database systems used in libraries usually come to mind. These systems fall into two categories. First, there are the bibliographic citation retrieval systems, which include systems offered by Lockheed Corporation, Systems Development Corporation, and Bibliographic Retrieval Services, Inc. All of these systems provide access to large subject files, commonly termed *databases,* for on-line searching and the retrieval of citations pertinent to searcher requests. Telecommunications networks like Telenet and Tymeshare provide for long-range access to these databases, which reside at a few central locations.

The other group of databases are those represented by systems that may be considered primarily as cooperative cataloging systems. These include the Ohio College Library Center (OCLC), the Research Libraries Information Network (RLIN, formerly known as BALLOTS), the Washington Library Network (WLN), and the University of Toronto Library Automation Systems (UTLAS). In these systems, there is long-distance sharing of cataloging information in computer files. Updating of the databases is achieved by data contributed to the database system by member libraries. The bibliographic citation, with relevant cataloging data, is the unit of information retrieved through the database system.

These database systems are a particular class or type of the larger family of database systems, as that term is used by computer specialists. Although this group of database systems is familiar to library users, such systems require multiple subscribers for their support; other forms of database systems may be supported economically by only a single computer installation. The latter systems are flexible enough to contain many types of information other than bibliographic records. As libraries turn increasingly to on-line and information retrieval uses of their computer systems, it appears quite likely that they will become more involved with alternative forms of database systems.

The objective of this chapter is to approach database systems from a general standpoint. What are database systems? What do they do? Why should librarians and the library computer staff be aware of them? After these questions have been addressed, the specific kinds of database systems that librarians are already familiar with will be discussed.

THE DATABASE CONCEPT

In order to comprehend the database concept, it is necessary to review the history of the earliest computerized data-processing systems. The file organization of these systems was simple. It had developed directly from those large manual systems that preceded the advent of computer technology. The files were *flat files*, in which records occurred one after the other. The formats in which individual records were laid out were discussed extensively in Chapter 3. The earliest systems used the simplest record layout—fixed-length records with fixed-length fields. Sample flat files are illustrated in Figure 46.

Late in the 1960s, it was discovered that more complicated forms of file organization could lead to more efficient data storage and more effective data usage. The more complicated file structures were based on the introduction of logical relationships between various records in one or more files. A *logical relationship* could be created between two records by a systems program that would maintain the relationship between the records. Thus, an applications program that would retrieve one of the records would have a convenient methodology for retrieving or manipulating

FLAT FILES

On Cards   On Tape

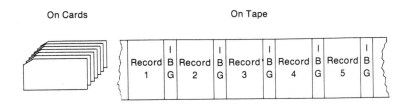

Figure 46 FLAT FILES CONSIST OF RECORDS OCCURRING
CONSECUTIVELY AND IN A KNOWN SEQUENCE.

that record's associated or related records. In this manner, the
building and maintenance of interrelationships between records
in one or more files resulted in database file organization.

A major characteristic of database systems is that, due to the introduction of logical relationships among records, the data of a
computing system may be more highly centralized. Data that
had been stored in numerous, totally independent flat files could
now be combined into one large database system. Database file
organization allows combining what would be many separate flat
files into one all-inclusive file system—the database—resulting in
reduced data redundancy.

Figures 47 and 48 may serve to clarify this situation. Figure 47
illustrates the collection of logically and physically separate flat
files that would be maintained in a heavily automated library's
computing system. Figure 48 illustrates the database concept.
Here there is only one large file, the database, which contains all
the machine-readable information in the system.

There are three main approaches to implementing the database
concept through computer software. In the *own-language* approach, there is a special language that must be used for all communications with the database. All information seeking in or updating of the database must be done through the database's own
language for interaction.

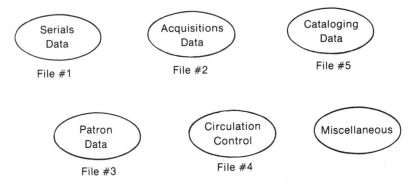

Figure 47   AN EXAMPLE OF LIBRARY FLAT FILES.

The second software method allows users to respond to queries from an on-line interactive program. Users interact with the database in terms of fairly restrictive fill-in-the-blank responses.

In the third software implementation of databases, computer programs are written in standard programming languages such as COBOL and PL/I. These *host languages* interface with the database through standard database systems programs provided as a part of the database software package.

The systems that librarians are most familiar with—accessing databases through terminal teleprocessing—fall into the first category. Specific systems have their own particular self-contained languages for database interaction and data retrieval,

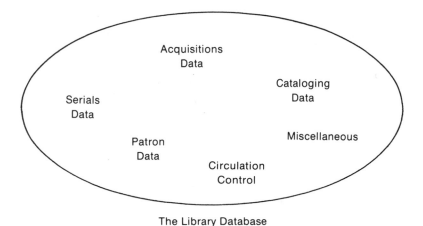

The Library Database

Figure 48   LIBRARY DATABASE FILE ORGANIZATION.

for example, Systems Development Corporation's ORBIT and Lockheed's DIALOG. But in interactions with the databases via these languages, it should be realized that searcher responses to system questions usually are restricted to a very limited and well-defined range of choices. A certain tendency toward the fill-in-the-forms approach is evident in these systems as well.

Clearly, these self-contained methods for database usage have some important advantages over the host-language method. The languages used by the searcher in database query systems are fairly simple. One can learn them in a few days from associates or at formal training sessions. No computer programmers are required except at the central system headquarters. In other words, there is some programming involved, but the users need not be concerned with it.

On the other hand, the self-contained approaches lack a certain flexibility. The bibliographic citation retrieval systems in use are designed specifically for that purpose. An automation project at a hypothetical library involving the file consolidation shown in Figure 48 cannot be attempted through the use of the database query system which is in place; local database software is required for this.

The host-language approach is the most flexible software method for implementating database systems. Host-language packages are widely available for purchase by computer installations. In business computing, they are fairly common where total data storage requirements are large and file complexity is great; their use in libraries is currently spreading. Here the discussion will focus on what these database systems are, what they can do, why they are useful, what advantages they offer library automation systems, and how they are similar to and different from the databases accessed through the library's subscription to a terminal.

HOST-LANGUAGE DATABASE SYSTEMS

In a host-language system, a programming language such as COBOL or PL/I is used for all interactions with the database. Programs written in these languages may be either batch-mode or on-line. But the important point is that the programs written in host languages are necessary for interaction with the database. In all of these host-language database systems, programs request services of database systems programs in order to access the database. The database systems programs are contacted via regular or standard methods for program interfacing. Normal modes of interprogram communications are followed. Programmers do require some training to learn how and when to make requests of the system through their host-language programs, however. The database systems programs are purchased as an integral part of the database software package.

The advantage of the host-language approach is the flexibility it provides computer installations to create their own database systems. The sort of library automation database pictured in Figure 48 is feasible when using a host-language database package. In this example, all data in library computer system files is combined into a single database.

Popular purchasable database software systems are of the host-language type. They include IMS, TOTAL, ADABAS, System 2000, IDMS, and Datacom and Model 204.[1] Due to the prohibitive expense involved in creating one's own database systems software, most database system users purchase their database system. This is not true of those own-language subscription services for libraries mentioned earlier, which are different by virtue of not being local, on-site systems.

Host-language systems can be divided into three basic categories: hierarchical, network, and inverted file.[2] These categories

[1]Addresses for the vendors of these database systems are:

    IMS–IBM, contact the nearest office.

    TOTAL.–Cincom Systems, 2300 Montana Avenue, Cincinnati, Ohio 45211.

    ADABAS–Software AG of North America, Reston International Center, 11800 Sunrise Valley Drive, Reston, Virginia 22091.

System 2000–Intel Commercial Systems Division, P.O. Box 9968, Austin, Texas 78766.

    IDMS–Cullinane Corporation, 20 William Street, Wellesley, Massachusetts 02181.

    Datacom–Applied Data Research, Route 206 and Orchard Road, CN-8, Princeton, New Jersey 08540.

Model 204–Computer Corporation of America, 575 Technology Square, Cambridge, Massachusetts 02139.

[2]A fourth category of database system, relational databases, is presently being developed in numerous research centers across the country. At the time of this writing, however, no relational systems are commercially available.

reflect the fundamental organization of the database file structures. The basic differences among the three systems relate to the sort of file structure each one offers. Each will be described in turn by focusing on specific sample systems.

Hierarchical Database Systems

In hierarchical database systems the logical record is called a *database record*. Each database record is composed of units referred to as *segments,* which are arranged in a hierarchical or tree structure (see Figure 49). The fundamental principle of this hierarchical structure is that each segment is qualified in successively narrower terms, from the topmost segment, down through succeeding segments, to the subject segment. Thus, the hierarchical structure enforces logical relationships among the segments in a database record.

In Figure 49, segment number 1 at the top of the database record is the *root segment*. All segments below the root segment are its *dependent segments*. Each segment numbered in the diagram is a different *segment type*. Each segment type is differentiated by its own record format, similar to the record layouts of the logical records described in Chapter 3. In other words, each segment type can

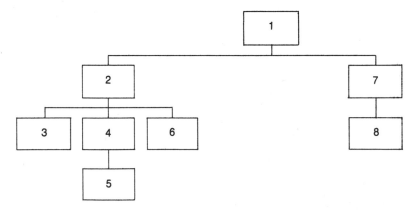

Figure 49   AN EXAMPLE OF A HIERARCHICAL DATABASE RECORD.

contain certain predefined information fields. Different segment types have different relative positions in the inverted-tree structure of the database record.

An important point is that there may be many occurrences of a particular segment type within the tree. This is called *twinning*. Figure 50 shows multiple occurrences of segment type 2. Twinning is always assumed to be possible for any segment in the logical database record. Twinning is not shown in an illustration such as Figure 49 by convention, for reasons of clarity.

It is also possible that there may not be any occurrences for a given segment type in a given database record. For example, some database records might not have any occurrences of segments 2 or 8, even though their logical structure dictates that they could have occurrences of these segment types. When a segment type is not present, it is clear that no segments dependent on it are present either. In Figure 49, for example, if a particular database record does not have an occurrence of a segment of type 2, it cannot have occurrences of dependent segments of types 3, 4, 5, or 6.

The result is that the database record is the logical record of a database file; it is composed of segment types, each having its own record format and containing its own kinds of data. There may be multiple occurrences of a given segment type in a database record, called *twins*. The segment is the unit of data read into or written from an applications program in a single I/O operation. But it is the group of segments together that compose a logical or database record.

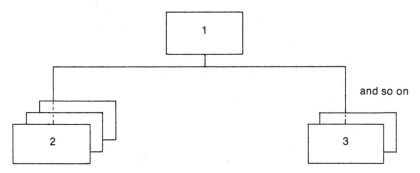

Figure 50 TWINNING (MULTIPLE OCCURRENCES OF A GIVEN SEGMENT TYPE.)

There are many finer points of database record structure of interest to librarians. Figure 51 diagrams a bibliographic record in one possible database record format. It can be seen that the MAIN ENTRY has been declared as the record root. Different segments represent different types of data that would be associated with a single occurrence of this root. For each segment type, there could be multiple segment occurrences. For example, for a single MAIN ENTRY, there may be more than one author and, thus, an AUTHOR segment twin chain; frequently, there will be an ADDED ENTRIES twin chain. Usually, there will be only single occurrences of the IMPRINT and COLLATION segments in a database record. Notice how there are dependent segments to the IMPRINT segment; this segment might be referred to as the *parent* to its *dependent segments* or *children*. The IMPRINT segment itself is a root to its own *subtree* within the MAIN ENTRY database record.

IMS: IMS, or the Information Management System, is a hierarchical-type database system written and sold by IBM. It follows the general outline of the hierarchical database record structure just provided. Various forms of IMS include IMS/360, for Series 360 computers; IMS/VS,[3] for System/370 OS machines; and DOS/VS[4] DL/I,[5] for System/370 DOS systems. In all cases, DL/I is the name of the program component of the database software package. IMS is the single most widespread database system in use today.

Through its DL/I component, IMS provides comprehensive database management facilities for the host-language programs using it. Individual segments can be inserted, deleted, or replaced within a database record; furthermore, IMS can keep segment occurrences within the twin chains ordered, if so desired. Segment occurrences to be ordered may have either unique or nonunique keys, but they can be ordered only in ascending sequence.

IMS databases require DASDS as their storage devices; IMS provides direct access to segments having specified keys. IMS can provide either direct access by key or sequential access to any root or dependent segments desired. The actual accesses permitted for

[3] IMS/VS stands for Information Management System/Virtual Storage.
[4] DOS/VS stands for Disk Operating System/Virtual Storage.
[5] DL/I stands for Data Language/One.

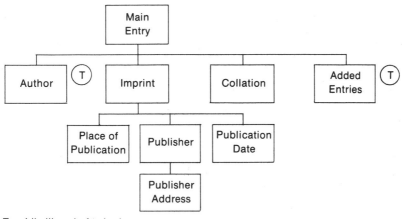

T = Likelihood of twinning
for this segment type

Figure 51   A BIBLIOGRAPHIC RECORD IN ONE POSSIBLE DATABASE FORMAT.

any segment type are specified by the installation using IMS by a procedure called database definition generation (DBDGEN). This process first sets up an IMS database by defining the structure of a database record, its dependent segments, sequencing or key fields, segment data formats, types of accesses desired for individual segment types, the access methods used for the database, and many other characteristics for an individual database. Therefore, DBDGEN is the procedure by which a computer installation defines the database that it wishes to create. Once the database definition has been generated, host-language applications programs are used to manipulate and process data in the database. DBDGEN is performed again only if the *database administrator*, the systems analyst in charge of the database, decides to make changes in the crucial characteristics of the database.

DBDGEN is a very important procedure from the standpoint of design considerations. It is through this procedure that the library computer installation using IMS fits its particular application to IMS software and the database concept. The skill of systems personnel in designing the database through DBDGEN is critical to successful use of the database system package in the library programming environment.

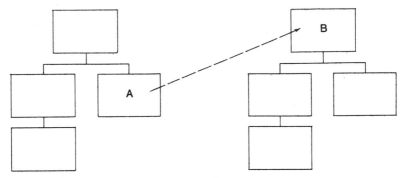

Figure 52   A LOGICAL RELATIONSHIP IN AN IMS DATABASE
SYSTEM.

IMS Features: At this point, a few features of ıмs can be mentioned, which have been selected to illustrate the power of database systems versus traditional flat files. One such feature is the
logical relationship. In ıмs, a logical relationship provides a *path*
from one specified segment to another. Such a path is drawn in
Figure 52 as a broken line from one segment pointing to another.
This means a computer program that has accessed the segment
labelled A can directly access segment B if it so desires.

   Logical relationships provide much more flexibility for processing of the database by applications programs. There are many different forms of logical relationships. As an example, Figure 53
shows two symmetrical-looking logical relationships within a

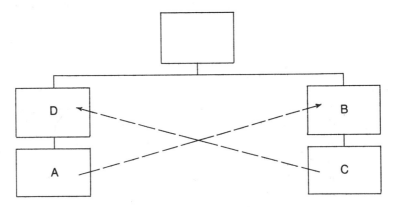

Figure 53   A LOGICAL RELATIONSHIP WITHIN A SINGLE IMS
DATABASE RECORD.

single database record. The basic purpose of logical relationships, which are defined at DBDGEN time, is to provide more flexibility in processing. Complicated logical relationships between different segments, other than those inherent in the database record's hierarchical structure, can be defined through the provision for logical relationships.

Secondary indexes are another powerful feature of IMS. These indexes allow direct access to segments based on keys other than those specified for the regular database record structure. In addition, secondary indexes can be used to make a database record appear to an applications program as if it has a totally different hierarchical or logical structure. Secondary indexes may be either much more convenient to use or otherwise better than the actual logical tree structure defined at DBDGEN time under certain processing conditions. In any case, the power and flexibility that this feature offers applications programs are quite significant.

As a final comment, the fullest form of the IMS database system, which is IMS/VS, offers facilities for variable-length segments. Depending on intended library use of the database, this could be an advantage to IMS.

TOTAL DATABASE NETWORK

TOTAL is representative of database systems having the network file organization. TOTAL is a product of CINCOM systems.

As a host-language database system, TOTAL is similar to IMS in some respects. TOTAL, too, provides system software to interface between applications programs and the database itself. DML (Data Management Language) is this interface software, rather than IMS' DL/I. Also, TOTAL has an equivalent to DBDGEN for initially defining crucial database characteristics. Database Definition Language (DBDL) is provided by TOTAL for this purpose. The basic difference between TOTAL and IMS is that TOTAL has a network organization for the database; information in the database is not hierarchically organized.

In the TOTAL network, there are datasets or files that are related logically only when defined during the DBDL procedure.

There are no segments that are automatically related into hierarchical structures by the requirements of a hierarchical database organization. Traditional flat files are related, as defined during DBDL, by *paths* and are referred to as *chained* together. A *chain* is simply a provision of an access path, permitting an applications program that has retrieved one data record to directly retrieve the record to which it is chained. In other words, it is a logical relationship between two records of files in the database.

TOTAL classifies all files as either master files or variable files.[6] A master file's logical records can be accessed directly as through a key, or in a sequential manner. An example would be a patron data file accessed by a patron identification number. A variable file is a dependent dataset and must be associated with one or more master datasets. Variable-file records are chained together in groups, each of which is chained to an appropriate master-file record (dependent on a master record key). As an example, logical records in the variable file might be individual borrowed items. Appropriate items borrowed would be chained to the proper patron identification number record in the master file.

The network concept develops from the multiple chains allowed between files. Master files may be associated with more than one variable file, and vice versa. All such relationships are specified by the database administrator during the DBDL procedure. Thus, TOTAL networking develops simple flat files into a sophisticated database network. As with hierarchical database structures and methodology, the purpose is to reduce data redundancy for all data contained in the computer's files, which permits more sophisticated computerized data processing.

Inverted Files

Inverted-file database systems represent the third major form of host-language systems. In this method, there are no logical records in the traditional sense. What is stored in the database is

[6] NOTE: Variable files have nothing to do with variable-length records. Variable-length records are not supported by TOTAL.

character-format text, such as bibliographic references, para-
graphs, abstracts, or journal articles. For searching purposes, a
number of indexes are built above the database file. A *data diction-
ary* lists data items (possibly words) and chains them to corresponding entries in the *occurrence index*. The occurrence index gives
the number of occurrences for the associated data items in the
database. A *data index* then provides actual locations of all data
elements in the database.

Inverted files are quite different in their aims and principles
from the other two database organizational methods discussed.
Used for text retrieval systems, inverted files are oriented toward
retrieval speed and Boolean-format search arguments. Due to the
emphasis on response time, other features of database organization are sacrificed. Insertion of data or addition of information to
the file may cost significantly in terms of software overhead.
Reorganization of the file for greater efficiency may be a time-
consuming proposition. Many inverted-file systems are device-
dependent—they cannot be easily moved to other installations or
to different storage devices in the same installation. Clearly, inverted files have a different orientation and purpose than do hierarchical and network database systems. Inverted files are organized for fast inquiry searching and place this goal above all
others.

ADABAS is one commercially marketed inverted-file system. As
the reader may already know, inverted-file database organization
is used in the internal operations of the popular bibliographic citation retrieval systems mentioned earlier in the chapter. SDC,
MEDLINE, Lockheed, and others all operate as inverted-file database systems.

It is quite likely that library use of subscription-service database
systems based on inverted-file structures will continue its current
expansion. Possibly, libraries will design their own local text retrieval systems as well.

EVALUATION

The reader should now be familiar with the general types of database file organizations and how they are implemented through

software. What are the advantages of database systems for library automation?

As shown in Figure 48, in a database situation, a number of traditional files are combined into one library database. A procedure such as DBDGEN or DBDL is used to define the nature of this database. Thus, the most important advantage of the database approach is that it is compatible with the *total-systems* method. The total-systems approach argues for a unified and coherent view of computer systems design. This software engineering theory seeks some sort of conceptual integrity for the disparate functional subsystems coexisting in a single computing system. Acquisitions, cataloging, and circulation control may be functionally different library subsystems, but all of these should be considered as parts in the larger library computing system, which must have some coherence or integrity within itself. Database systems foster this attitude in their provision for a single database file, rather than many individual flat files. Database file organization readily lends itself to the ''single-system'' theory.

Both the single-system philosophy and database software have been used successfully by a number of libraries. This is true in spite of the fact that articles in the literature of library automation often discuss only one particular functional library system as their topic. Too commonly, books on library automation assume an approach that emphasizes subsystems at the expense of the single-system approach. In these cases, chapters are entitled Acquisitions, Cataloging Systems, Serials, Circulation Control, Administrative Data Processing, and so forth.

Database systems, in addition to the advantage of the total-system concept, offer other benefits as well. Many of these advantages result from the centralization of all files into a single larger file—the reduction of data redundancy. And data can be made available to a wider range of applications programs than was previously possible. Files are not restricted to use by a particular group of programs; this is referred to as *data independence*.

Centralization of the data means that centralized control can be exercised, data integrity is increased, and a global view of the data is more readily obtainable. Clearly, maintaining or updating data is easier for a single database than for many disparate files.

For any database system, the database design and the definition/generation process are critical. It is important that experienced employees direct these particular operations: Programmers may need some training too. A final possible disadvantage to database systems is that they do involve the expense of complexity. For smaller systems, or those that are fairly simple or straightforward, the additional complexity involved in database software and organization may not be worthwhile.

These, then, are some of the characteristics of database systems. Given their increasing popularity and use for the past 10 years, it is important that librarians understand their principles and the ways in which they may be applied to library computing systems.

CHAPTER 11

Mini- and Microcomputer Systems

Minicomputers were introduced to libraries at the time of their early commercial marketing in the late 1960s. Minicomputer systems in libraries became widespread in the 1970s, and the significance of the minicomputer has been recognized in library automation literature.[1] These small and versatile computers are quite affordable for both general-purpose and dedicated library functions, and, as their purchase prices continue to drop, their sophistication and value will increase. With each passing year, it becomes more important that persons employed in libraries appreciate the capabilities of these smaller computers and understand their limitations as well.

Due to the unbelievable pace of technological change in the field of small computer systems, any discussion in a book such as this one is foredoomed to a degree of obsolescence even during its publication. But some description of the nature of small computer systems, their fundamental characteristics, and their significance

[1] See, for example:

A. N. Grosch. *Minicomputers in Libraries, 1979–1980.* White Plains, N.Y., Knowledge Industry Publications, 1979.

Proceedings of the 1974 Clinic on Library Applications of Data Processing: Applications of Minicomputers to Library and Related Problems. Edited by F. W. Lancaster. Urbana-Champaign, University of Illinois, 1974.

M. J. Young, F. A. Pessanite, and J. C. Reisinger. *Introduction to Minicomputers in Federal Libraries.* Washington, D.C., Library of Congress, 1978.

is mandatory, because an ever-increasing role is apparent for small computer systems for both general use and libraries specifically.

To discuss minicomputers in general terms, most analysts of computing trends agree that the introduction of commercial minicomputing systems has had two effects on the overall computing market. First, minicomputers have taken some business away from the less-sophisticated mainframe market. If a company wanted a computer during the mid-1960s, it had only one option—to buy or rent a small mainframe, regardless of the limited nature of the company's requirement for computing power. The introduction of minicomputers offered businesses an alternative to purchasing an underused mainframe. A company with requirements for small-scale computer use now has the option of obtaining a much lower priced computing system. Minicomputers have allowed the purchase of lesser systems for lesser needs. To place this principle within the context of the present time, however, many current minicomputers have developed sufficient technology to offer far more computing power than the typical mainframes of the mid-1960s.

The second effect that minicomputer sales have had on the computer industry is closely associated with the first. In addition to competing for sales with the smaller mainframes, minicomputers have extended computing power to a whole new group of first-time computer users. Many organizations previously unable to afford the capabilities of computers now have full-fledged, although sometimes limited, computing systems.

Simultaneously, libraries have benefited from both effects of the commercial marketing of minicomputers. Generally, libraries are on the smaller end of the computing market. Thus, as a group, libraries especially have benefited from the continuing development of small computing systems.

For all the promise that minicomputers offer to libraries and other small-system users, however, an exact definition of minicomputers is elusive. A computer's word size is one criterion for defining minicomputers. Word size, the reader will recall, is the unit of information upon which CPU architecture is based. Most mainframes, for example, have a word size of 32 bits (four eight-bit bytes). This word size does not include any check bits, which are of internal use in electronic accuracy verification only. Minicomputers tend to have a 16-bit word size. Although word size is about as accurate a criterion as any for separating minicomputers from mainframes, it should not be taken as definitive. For example, a recent trend has been to upgrade minicomputer architecture to mainframe scale by expanding word size to a full 32 bits, resulting in the so-called ''superminis.'' Sales of these ''superminis'' in the late 1970s indicated a demand for high-powered minicomputers; therefore, the traditional line drawn between different sizes of computers continues to fade.

Minicomputers can be defined by other characteristics. Price range is one, since minis certainly cost less than mainframe systems. In addition to being a volatile measurement, however, computing system prices often depend as much on I/O and storage device prices as on the computer itself. The I/O bus is another distinguishing feature of minicomputers. The I/O bus is the architectural method for connection of the minicomputer to its associated peripheral devices.

Some minicomputer features mentioned elsewhere in this book include the relative sophistication of their operating systems, their forms of memory management, their limited systems support software, and their core capacity, among others.

Rather than attempt to further define minicomputers, a few central characteristics that indicate the relative value of minicomputer systems will be discussed. These variable features serve to distinguish minicomputers from one another and from mainframes.

First, minicomputers and their systems components often are designed for specific purposes. Some minis are built specifically for numerical control programming; in this capacity, they may automatically control manufacturing processes as varied as steel production or tool die etching. Process control has been a very popular use of minis.

Second, minicomputers have been useful in mathematical programming situations. They can, for example, direct the operations of a nuclear reactor or lend computing support to an engineering group. Other minicomputers have been sold as teleprocessing systems for small companies. These systems support a number of on-line CRTs for data entry and are used for accounting purposes and order processing.

Point-of-sale systems are oriented toward saving and analyzing transaction data as the transactions occur. This use of minicomputers is very similar to their use for circulation control systems in libraries. In a business situation, the light-wand and bar-coded labels provide transaction data on groceries or other salable items; in the library, they provide data on books, periodicals, and other borrowable items.

It is apparent that minicomputers have found application to a large range of problems. It should be recognized that the intended use of particular minicomputers may have had a profound influence on the design of these computers and their systems. Some systems are on-line and/or teleprocessing oriented; others are designed for batch-mode users. Some are created for dedicated use only, while others are intended for more general functions. The library would not want to pay a premium for such mathematical refinements as 32-bit accuracy or floating-point registers. The important point is that minicomputers are smaller than mainframes in purpose and orientation, as well as in size and price. While mainframes offer large-capacity, general-purpose computing power, minicomputer manufacturers tend to select a target group of potential users and build a machine and system for its needs. Persons in libraries must always be aware of the orientation of a minicomputer system and how this system relates to library processing needs. Many minicomputers will not be as adaptable to library requirements as general-purpose mainframes. On the other hand, certain minicomputer systems designed for library or similar use are ideal for the library or information retrieval programming environment. Since library needs can be very different from those of industrial computer users, library personnel must carefully consider how certain special-purpose minicomputer systems address their processing requirements.

Closely related to these issues is the question of the software available for a minicomputer system. In the relatively young world of minicomputing, software tends to distinguish systems and their potential use much more than hardware does. How sophisticated is the operating system, and what is its approach to memory management? Clearly, a uniprogramming system is quite different from one featuring multiprogramming with static-partitioned memory management. And what about support software? Does the system offer programmers on-line debugging and testing software, batch-mode debugging, or none of these features? How about text editors, on-line data entry, access methods, sorting utilities, and other support software? Investigation of a minicomputer system's software reveals much more about that system and its capabilities than does the hardware.

The support of programming languages provides another test of how well many minicomputer systems relate to library needs. Some minicomputers offer only FORTRAN. Often a somewhat streamlined ANSI (American National Standards Institute) standard compiler, this FORTRAN may have absolutely no string-manipulation features. The library might find the language difficult or impossible to use in information storage and retrieval applications. Some minis offer COBOL, BASIC, or other programming languages. These may be more or less useful to the library, depending on their completeness and the library's intended use of its computer. PL/I is available for very few minicomputers. The problem in implementing PL/I on a minicomputer is that the original mainframe compiler required 180K in which to run (most other languages require only 120K), and it is difficult to scale the PL/I compiler down to the memory resource capacity of many minicomputer systems.

One other important aspect of minicomputer systems is the service support provided by the various manufacturers. Equipment, and even software availability, are often lesser determinants in minicomputer sales than the extent and nature of the service backup provided for these systems. Most analysts agree that it has been the manufacturers' level of support and service that has distinguished the best-selling minicomputer models from the rest.

MINICOMPUTER SUMMARY

In this brief discussion, a few of the main factors of which librarians will want to be cognizant in considering and evaluating minicomputer systems have been reviewed. The purpose(s) for which a system is designed, the software support available, and the service network are all significant variables. Interested readers are urged to consult current periodicals[2] for more specific information.

MICROCOMPUTER SYSTEMS

Microcomputers were invented in the early 1970s, and marketing began in the mid-1970s. These computers resulted from a number of technological advances, the most important of which was the development of *metal-on-silicon* (MOS) or *microchip* technology. Each *chip* is about the size of a postage stamp and constitutes an entire CPU. Referred to as a *microprocessor,* a chip is a complete CPU without the memory or other external parts of the computer. The most amazing aspect of these CPUs is their price—most microprocessors cost between $15 and $30.[3] Various forms of these microchips have been made into different microprocessors and forms of memory as well. A memory chip might store, for example, anywhere from 1/2K to more than 64Kbytes of information. A byte, incidentally, corresponds to the word size of most microcomputers. Microprocessors with two-byte and four-byte word sizes are presently becoming available.

Microchip technology was fundamental to the development of microcomputers. The silicon technology defines this class of computers. But other technologies as well were essential to their development. Small disk drives with nonrigid disks were invented. These *floppy disks* come in 5-1/4" and 8" sizes and may hold anywhere from 70Kbytes to many hundred kilobytes of data each. The traditional hard disks also have become available for

---

[2]Major periodicals of the computing industry include: *Computerworld, Information Systems News, Infosystems, Datamation, Computer Decisions,* and many others. Those publications specializing in coverage of minicomputers and microcomputers include: *Mini-Micro Systems, Infoworld, Byte, Creative Computing, Interface Age, Kilobaud, Small Business Computers Magazine,* and *onComputing.*

[3]This price is for the microprocessor chip only. Complete microcomputer systems cost $500 or more and are very limited in computing capacity until one reaches outlays of $1,000 to $8,000.

use in microcomputing systems. As mentioned earlier, paper tape enjoyed a brief resurgence as a microcomputer I/O methodology and storage medium. Cassette tapes are another form of storage medium for these smallest computing systems.

At this time, the first microcomputer systems for small businesses are being developed and marketed. The indisputable advantage to these systems is their cost. Because of their exceptionally low price, microcomputers may have effects on the computer market analogous to those that minicomputers had. Microcomputers may introduce a whole new group of smallest-system users to computing and, at the same time, steal business away from the lesser end of the minicomputer market.

For the present, however, microcomputers still present serious problems for computing applications in business and libraries. For example, their reliability is highly suspect. One can purchase a floppy disk drive for less than $600, but how long it will work is the buyer's unguaranteed guess. Another important concern is the lack of service for microcomputers. Some industry observers suggest that service networks for microcomputers will grow in time, the same as they did for minicomputers. Others feel that retail stores will provide service and support. And still others maintain that the computer industry's profits on these systems will prove insufficient to warrant and support such service networks. At the present time, the only certainty is that libraries and other organizations cannot afford to depend on these systems unless professional repair service is available for them.[4]

Finally, it should be noted that microcomputer software development is still in its infancy. Operating systems are primitive, utility programs are rare, and programming languages are only now being developed. Concerning programming languages, many microcomputer manufacturers offer only the difficult assembly languages and limited versions of BASIC and FORTRAN. Independent software vendors are creating and selling more powerful versions of BASIC and ANSI-standard FORTRAN and COBOL. Other industrially oriented languages, such as C, PASCAL, and APL,

---

[4]An introduction to microcomputers for librarians may be found in H. Fosdick, "The Microcomputer Revolution," *Library Journal, 105*(13):1467–1472, July 1980.

are presently in various stages of release and development. PL/1, in which librarians should be particularly interested, exists in two versions. These are referred to as PL/M and PL/I-80. Both versions retain the major string-manipulation features of full PL/1, and both require fewer than 64Kbytes of memory. Again, the reader is reminded that up-to-date information in this area is best obtained from those computer industry periodicals mentioned earlier in this chapter.[2]

SUMMARY

Minicomputers developed from humble beginnings similar to those of today's microcomputers. Yet, within the brief span of a decade, minicomputers have become increasingly valuable to libraries. Microcomputers will do the same. They might also open new horizons in their provision of cheap processors, for example, in multiprocessing applications. At this time, it is impossible to predict where microtechnology will lead us. It is virtually assured, however, that librarians will encounter the results and benefits of microtechnology in the 1980s.

Appendix A:

Character Codes

CODE TRANSLATION TABLE ⑨

Dec.	Hex	Instruction (RR)	BCDIC	EBCDIC(1)	ASCII	7-Track Tape BCDIC(2)	Card Code EBCDIC	Binary
0	00			NUL	NUL		12-0-1-8-9	0000 0000
1	01			SOH	SOH		12-1-9	0000 0001
2	02			STX	STX		12-2-9	0000 0010
3	03			ETX	ETX		12-3-9	0000 0011
4	04	SPM		PF	EOT		12-4-9	0000 0100
5	05	BALR		HT	ENQ		12-5-9	0000 0101
6	06	BCTR		LC	ACK		12-6-9	0000 0110
7	07	BCR		DEL	BEL		12-7-9	0000 0111
8	08	SSK		GE	BS		12-8-9	0000 1000
9	09	ISK		RLF	HT		12-1-8-9	0000 1001
10	0A	SVC		SMM	LF		12-2-8-9	0000 1010
11	0B			VT	VT		12-3-8-9	0000 1011
12	0C			FF	FF		12-4-8-9	0000 1100
13	0D			CR	CR		12-5-8-9	0000 1101
14	0E	MVCL		SO	SO		12-6-8-9	0000 1110
15	0F	CLCL		SI	SI		12-7-8-9	0000 1111
16	10	LPR		DLE	DLE		12-11-1-8-9	0001 0000
17	11	LNR		DC1	DC1		11-1-9	0001 0001
18	12	LTR		DC2	DC2		11-2-9	0001 0010
19	13	LCR		TM	DC3		11-3-9	0001 0011
20	14	NR		RES	DC4		11-4-9	0001 0100
21	15	CLR		NL	NAK		11-5-9	0001 0101
22	16	OR		BS	SYN		11-6-9	0001 0110
23	17	XR		IL	ETB		11-7-9	0001 0111
24	18	LR		CAN	CAN		11-8-9	0001 1000
25	19	CR		EM	EM		11-1-8-9	0001 1001
26	1A	AR		CC	SUB		11-2-8-9	0001 1010
27	1B	SR		CU1	ESC		11-3-8-9	0001 1011
28	1C	MR		IFS	FS		11-4-8-9	0001 1100
29	1D	DR		IGS	GS		11-5-8-9	0001 1101
30	1E	ALR		IRS	RS		11-6-8-9	0001 1110
31	1F	SLR		IUS	US		11-7-8-9	0001 1111
32	20	LPDR		DS	SP		11-0-1-8-9	0010 0000
33	21	LNDR		SOS	!		0-1-9	0010 0001
34	22	LTDR		FS	"		0-2-9	0010 0010
35	23	LCDR			#		0-3-9	0010 0011
36	24	HDR		BYP	$		0-4-9	0010 0100
37	25	LRDR		LF	%		0-5-9	0010 0101
38	26	MXR		ETB	&		0-6-9	0010 0110
39	27	MXDR		ESC	'		0-7-9	0010 0111
40	28	LDR			(		0-8-9	0010 1000
41	29	CDR			)		0-1-8-9	0010 1001
42	2A	ADR		SM	*		0-2-8-9	0010 1010
43	2B	SDR		CU2	+		0-3-8-9	0010 1011

SOURCE: Reprinted by permission from System/370 Reference Summary (Fourth Edition, November 1976, GX20-1850-3). Copyright 1976 by International Business Machines Corporation.

CODE TRANSLATION TABLE (Contd) ⑨

Dec.	Hex	Instruction (RR)	Graphics and Controls BCDIC EBCDIC(1) ASCII			7-Track Tape BCDIC(2)	Card Code EBCDIC	Binary
44	2C	MDR			,		0-4-8-9	0010 1100
45	2D	DDR		ENQ	-		0-5-8-9	0010 1101
46	2E	AWR		ACK	.		0-6-8-9	0010 1110
47	2F	SWR		BEL	/		0-7-8-9	0010 1111
48	30	LPER			0		12-11-0-1-8-9	0011 0000
49	31	LNER			1		1-9	0011 0001
50	32	LTER		SYN	2		2-9	0011 0010
51	33	LCER			3		3-9	0011 0011
52	34	HER		PN	4		4-9	0011 0100
53	35	LRER		RS	5		5-9	0011 0101
54	36	AXR		UC	6		6-9	0011 0110
55	37	SXR		EOT	7		7-9	0011 0111
56	38	LER			8		8-9	0011 1000
57	39	CER			9		1-8-9	0011 1001
58	3A	AER			:		2-8-9	0011 1010
59	3B	SER		CU3	;		3-8-9	0011 1011
60	3C	MER		DC4	<		4-8-9	0011 1100
61	3D	DER		NAK	=		5-8-9	0011 1101
62	3E	AUR			>		6-8-9	0011 1110
63	3F	SUR		SUB	?		7-8-9	.0011 1111

1. Two columns of EBCDIC graphics are shown. The first gives IBM standard U.S. bit pattern assignments. The second shows the T-11 and TN text printing chains (120 graphics).
2. Add C (check bit) for odd or even parity as needed, except as noted.
3. For even parity use CA.

TWO-CHARACTER BSC DATA LINK CONTROLS		
Function	EBCDIC	ASCII
ACK-0	DLE,X'70'	DLE,0
ACK-1	DLE,X'61'	DLE,1
WACK	DLE,X'6B'	DLE, ;
RVI	DLE,X'7C'	DLE,<

CODE TRANSLATION TABLE (Contd) ⑩

Dec.	Hex	Instruction (RX)	Graphics and Controls BCDIC EBCDIC(1) ASCII			7-Track Tape BCDIC(2)	Card Code EBCDIC	Binary
64	40	STH	Sp	Sp	@	(3)	no punches	0100 0000
65	41	LA			A		12-0-1-9	0100 0001
66	42	STC			B		12-0-2-9	0100 0010
67	43	IC			C		12-0-3-9	0100 0011
68	44	EX			D		12-0-4-9	0100 0100
69	45	BAL			E		12-0-5-9	0100 0101
70	46	BCT			F		12-0-6-9	0100 0110
71	47	BC			G		12-0-7-9	0100 0111
72	48	LH			H		12-0-8-9	0100 1000
73	49	CH			I		12-1-8	0100 1001
74	4A	AH	¢	¢	J		12-2-8	0100 1010
75	4B	SH	.	.	.	K	B A 8 2 1	12-3-8	0100 1011
76	4C	MH	¤)	<	<	L	B A 8 4	12-4-8	0100 1100
77	4D		[	(	(	M	B A 8 4 1	12-5-8	0100 1101
78	4E	CVD	<	+	+	N	B A 8 4 2	12-6-8	0100 1110
79	4F	CVB	‡	!	!	O	B A 8 4 2 1	12-7-8	0100 1111
80	50	ST	& +	&	&	P	B A	12	0101 0000
81	51				Q		12-11-1-9	0101 0001
82	52				R		12-11-2-9	0101 0010
83	53	.			S		12-11-3-9	0101 0011
84	54	N			T		12-11-4-9	0101 0100
85	55	CL			U		12-11-5-9	0101 0101
86	56	O			V		12-11-6-9	0101 0110
87	57	X			W		12-11-7-9	0101 0111

Continued on the following page

CODE TRANSLATION TABLE (Contd) ⑩

Dec.	Hex	Instruction (RX)	Graphics and Controls BCDIC	EBCDIC(1)	ASCII	7-Track Tape BCDIC(2)	Card Code EBCDIC	Binary
88	58	L			X		12-11-8-9	0101 1000
89	59	C			Y		11-1-8	0101 1001
90	5A	A		!	! Z		11-2-8	0101 1010
91	5B	S	$	$_	$ [	B 8 21	11-3-8	0101 1011
92	5C	M	•	•	• \	B 84	11-4-8	0101 1100
93	5D	D	]	)	)]	B 84 1	11-5-8	0101 1101
94	5E	AL	;	;	; ¬ ^	B 842	11-6-8	0101 1110
95	5F	SL	Δ	¬	¬ _	B 8421	11-7-8	0101 1111
96	60	STD	-	-	- `	B	11	0110 0000
97	61		/	/	/ a	A 1	0-1	0110 0001
98	62				b		11-0-2-9	0110 0010
99	63				c		11-0-3-9	0110 0011
100	64				d		11-0-4-9	0110 0100
101	65				e		11-0-5-9	0110 0101
102	66				f		11-0-6-9	0110 0110
103	67	MXD			g		11-0-7-9	0110 0111
104	68	LD			h		11-0-8-9	0110 1000
105	69	CD			i		0-1-8	0110 1001
106	6A	AD		!	j		12-11	0110 1010
107	6B	SD	,	,	, k	A 8 21	0-3-8	0110 1011
108	6C	MD	%(	%	% l	A 84	0-4-8	0110 1100
109	6D	DD	⋎	_	_ m	A 84 1	0-5-8	0110 1101
110	6E	AW	\	>	> n	A 842	0-6-8	0110 1110
111	6F	SW	⚹	?	? o	A 8421	0-7-8	0110 1111
112	70	STE			p		12-11-0	0111 0000
113	71				q		12-11-0-1-9	0111 0001
114	72				r		12-11-0-2-9	0111 0010
115	73				s		12-11-0-3-9	0111 0011
116	74				t		12-11-0-4-9	0111 0100
117	75				u		12-11-0-5-9	0111 0101
118	76				v		12-11-0-6-9	0111 0110
119	77				w		12-11-0-7-9	0111 0111
120	78	LE			x		12-11-0-8-9	0111 1000
121	79	CE			y		1-8	0111 1001
122	7A	AE	ᵗᵇ	:	: z	A	2-8	0111 1010
123	7B	SE	# •	#	# {	8 21	3-8	0111 1011
124	7C	ME	@ '	@	@ ¦	84	4-8	0111 1100
125	7D	DE	:	'	' }	84 1	5-8	0111 1101
126	7E	AU	>	▪	▪ ~	842	6-8	0111 1110
127	7F	SU	√	"	" DEL	8421	7-8	0111 1111

CODE TRANSLATION TABLE (Contd) ⑪

Dec.	Hex	Instruction and Format	Graphics and Controls BCDIC	EBCDIC(1)	ASCII	7-Track Tape BCDIC(2)	Card Code EBCDIC	Binary
128	80	SSM -S					12-0-1-8	1000 0000
129	81			a	a		12-0-1	1000 0001
130	82	LPSW -S		b	b		12-0-2	1000 0010
131	83	Diagnose		c	c		12-0-3	1000 0011
132	84	WRD }SI		d	d		12-0-4	1000 0100
133	85	RDD		e	e		12-0-5	1000 0101
134	86	BXH		f	f		12-0-6	1000 0110
135	87	BXLE		g	g		12-0-7	1000 0111
136	88	SRL		h	h		12-0-8	1000 1000
137	89	SLL		i	i		12-0-9	1000 1001
138	8A	SRA					12-0-2-8	1000 1010
139	8B	SLA }RS			{		12-0-3-8	1000 1011

CODE TRANSLATION TABLE (Contd) ⑪

Dec.	Hex	Instruction and Format	Graphics and Controls BCDIC	EBCDIC(1)	ASCII	7-Track Tape BCDIC(2)	Card Code EBCDIC	Binary
140	8C	SRDL		≤			12-0-4-8	1000 1100
141	8D	SLDL		(			12-0-5-8	1000 1101
142	8E	SRDA		+			12-0-6-8	1000 1110
143	8F	SLDA		+			12-0-7-8	1000 1111
144	90	STM ⎫					12-11-1-8	1001 0000
145	91	TM ⎬ SI	j	j			12-11-1	1001 0001
146	92	MVI ⎭	k	k			12-11-2	1001 0010
147	93	TS -S	l	l			12-11-3	1001 0011
148	94	NI ⎫	m	m			12-11-4	1001 0100
149	95	CLI ⎬ SI	n	n			12-11-5	1001 0101
150	96	OI ⎪	o	o			12-11-6	1001 0110
151	97	XI ⎭	p	p			12-11-7	1001 0111
152	98	LM -RS	q	q			12-11-8	1001 1000
153	99		r	r			12-11-9	1001 1001
154	9A						12-11-2-8	1001 1010
155	9B			}			12-11-3-8	1001 1011
156	9C	SIO, SIOF ⎫		⌐			12-11-4-8	1001 1100
157	9D	TIO, CLRIO ⎬ S		)			12-11-5-8	1001 1101
158	9E	HIO, HDV ⎪		±			12-11-6-8	1001 1110
159	9F	TCH ⎭		■			12-11-7-8	1001 1111
160	A0			‾			11-0-1-8	1010 0000
161	A1		~	°			11-0-1	1010 0001
162	A2		s	s			11-0-2	1010 0010
163	A3		t	t			11-0-3	1010 0011
164	A4		u	u			11-0-4	1010 0100
165	A5		v	v			11-0-5	1010 0101
166	A6		w	w			11-0-6	1010 0110
167	A7		x	x			11-0-7	1010 0111
168	A8		y	y			11-0-8	1010 1000
169	A9		z	z			11-0-9	1010 1001
170	AA						11-0-2-8	1010 1010
171	AB			∟			11-0-3-8	1010 1011
172	AC	STNSM ⎫ SI		┌			11-0-4-8	1010 1100
173	AD	STOSM ⎭		[			11-0-5-8	1010 1101
174	AE	SIGP -RS		≥			11-0-6-8	1010 1110
175	AF	MC -SI		●			11-0-7-8	1010 1111
176	B0			0			12-11-0-1-8	1011 0000
177	B1	LRA -RX		1			12-11-0-1	1011 0001
178	B2	See below		2			12-11-0-2	1011 0010
179	B3			3			12-11-0-3	1011 0011
180	B4			4			12-11-0-4	1011 0100
181	B5			5			12-11-0-5	1011 0101
182	B6	STCTL ⎫ RS		6			12-11-0-6	1011 0110
183	B7	LCTL ⎭		7			12-11-0-7	1011 0111
184	B8			8			12-11-0-8	1011 1000
185	B9			9			12-11-0-9	1011 1001
186	BA	CS ⎫ RS					12-11-0-2-8	1011 1010
187	BB	CDS ⎭		⌐			12-11-0-3-8	1011 1011
188	BC			¬			12-11-0-4-8	1011 1100
189	BD	CLM ⎫		]			12-11-0-5-8	1011 1101
190	BE	STCM ⎬ RS		‡			12-11-0-6-8	1011 1110
191	BF	ICM ⎭		¬			12-11-0-7-8	1011 1111

Op code (S format)

B202 - STIDP	B207 - STCKC	B20D - PTLB
B203 - STIDC	B208 - SPT	B210 - SPX
B204 - SCK	B209 - STPT	B211 - STPX
B205 - STCK	B20A - SPKA	B212 - STAP
B206 - SCKC	B20B - IPK	B213 - RRB

Continued on the following page

CODE TRANSLATION TABLE (Contd) ⑫

Dec.	Hex	Instruction (SS)	Graphics and Controls BCDIC	EBCDIC(1)	ASCII	7-Track Tape BCDIC(2)	Card Code EBCDIC	Binary
192	C0		?	{		B A 8 2	12-0	1100 0000
193	C1		A	A	A	B A 1	12-1	1100 0001
194	C2		B	B	B	B A 2	12-2	1100 0010
195	C3		C	C	C	B A 2 1	12-3	1100 0011
196	C4		D	D	D	B A 4	12-4	1100 0100
197	C5		E	E	E	B A 4 1	12-5	1100 0101
198	C6		F	F	F	B A 4 2	12-6	1100 0110
199	C7		G	G	G	B A 4 2 1	12-7	1100 0111
200	C8		H	H	H	B A 8	12-8	1100 1000
201	C9		I	I	I	B A 8 1	12-9	1100 1001
202	CA						12-0-2-8-9	1100 1010
203	CB						12-0-3-8-9	1100 1011
204	CC			⌠			12-0-4-8-9	1100 1100
205	CD						12-0-5-8-9	1100 1101
206	CE			Ψ			12-0-6-8-9	1100 1110
207	CF						12-0-7-8-9	1100 1111
208	D0		!	}		B 8 2	11-0	1101 0000
209	D1	MVN	J	J	J	B 1	11-1	1101 0001
210	D2	MVC	K	K	K	B 2	11-2	1101 0010
211	D3	MVZ	L	L	L	B 2 1	11-3	1101 0011
212	D4	NC	M	M	M	B 4	11-4	1101 0100
213	D5	CLC	N	N	N	B 4 1	11-5	1101 0101
214	D6	OC	O	O	O	B 4 2	11-6	1101 0110
215	D7	XC	P	P	P	B 4 2 1	11-7	1101 0111
216	D8		Q	Q	Q	B 8	11-8	1101 1000
217	D9		R	R	R	B 8 1	11-9	1101 1001
218	DA						12-11-2-8-9	1101 1010
219	DB						12-11-3-8-9	1101 1011
220	DC	TR					12-11-4-8-9	1101 1100
221	DD	TRT					12-11-5-8-9	1101 1101
222	DE	ED					12-11-6-8-9	1101 1110
223	DF	EDMK					12-11-7-8-9	1101 1111
224	E0		‡	\		A 8 2	0-2-8	1110 0000
225	E1						11-0-1-9	1110 0001
226	E2		S	S	S	A 2	0-2	1110 0010
227	E3		T	T	T	A 2 1	0-3	1110 0011
228	E4		U	U	U	A 4	0-4	1110 0100
229	E5		V	V	V	A 4 1	0-5	1110 0101
230	E6		W	W	W	A 4 2	0-6	1110 0110
231	E7		X	X	X	A 4 2 1	0-7	1110 0111
232	E8		Y	Y	Y	A 8	0-8	1110 1000
233	E9		Z	Z	Z	A 8 1	0-9	1110 1001
234	EA						11-0-2-8-9	1110 1010
235	EB						11-0-3-8-9	1110 1011
236	EC			⊣			11-0-4-8-9	1110 1100
237	ED						11-0-5-8-9	1110 1101
238	EE						11-0-6-8-9	1110 1110
239	EF						11-0-7-8-9	1110 1111
240	F0	SRP	0	0	0	8 2	0	1111 0000
241	F1	MVO	1	1	1	1	1	1111 0001
242	F2	PACK	2	2	2	2	2	1111 0010
243	F3	UNPK	3	3	3	2 1	3	1111 0011
244	F4		4	4	4	4	4	1111 0100
245	F5		5	5	5	4 1	5	1111 0101
246	F6		6	6	6	4 2	6	1111 0110
247	F7		7	7	7	4 2 1	7	1111 0111
248	F8	ZAP	8	8	8	8	8	1111 1000
249	F9	CP	9	9	9	8 1	9	1111 1001
250	FA	AP					12-11-0-2-8-9	1111 1010
251	FB	SP					12-11-0-3-8-9	1111 1011

CODE TRANSLATION TABLE (Contd)

(12)

Dec.	Hex	Instruction (SS)	Graphics and Controls BCDIC EBCDIC(1) ASCII		7-Track Tape BCDIC(2)	Card Code EBCDIC	Binary
252	FC	M P				12-11-0-4-8-9	1111 1100
253	FD	D P				12-11-0-5-8-9	1111 1101
254	FE					12-11-0-6-8-9	1111 1110
255	FF			EO		12-11-0-7-8-9	1111 1111

ANSI-DEFINED PRINTER CONTROL CHARACTERS
(A in RECFM field of DCB)

Code	Action before printing record
blank	Space 1 line
0	Space 2 lines
-	Space 3 lines
+	Suppress space
1	Skip to line 1 on new page

Appendix B:

IBM 3330 Disk Reference Summary Card

Capacity Table

Bytes per Record						Records Per	
Without Keys		With Keys				3336 Model 1 Pack	3336 Model 11 Pack
Min	Max	Min	Max	Trk	Cylinder		
6448	13030	6392	12974	1	19	7676	15352
4254	6447	4198	6391	2	38	15352	30704
3157	4253	3101	4197	3	57	23028	46056
2499	3156	2443	3100	4	76	30704	61408
2060	2498	2004	2442	5	95	38380	76760
1746	2059	1690	2003	6	114	46056	92112
1511	1745	1455	1689	7	133	53732	107464
1328	1510	1272	1454	8	152	61408	122816
1182	1327	1126	1271	9	171	69084	138168
1062	1181	1006	1125	10	190	76760	153520
963	1061	907	1005	11	209	84436	168872
878	962	822	906	12	228	92112	184224
806	877	750	821	13	247	99788	199576
743	805	687	749	14	266	107464	214928
688	742	632	686	15	285	115140	230280
640	687	584	631	16	304	122816	245632
597	639	541	583	17	323	130492	260984
558	596	502	540	18	342	138168	276336
524	557	468	501	19	361	145844	291688
492	523	436	467	20	380	153520	307040
464	491	408	435	21	399	161196	322392
438	463	382	407	22	418	168872	337744
414	437	358	381	23	437	176548	353096
392	413	336	357	24	456	184224	368448
372	391	316	335	25	475	191900	383800
353	371	297	315	26	494	199576	399152
336	352	280	296	27	513	207252	414504
319	335	263	279	28	532	214928	429856
304	318	248	262	29	551	222604	445208
290	303	234	247	30	570	230280	460560
277	289	221	233	31	589	237956	475912
264	276	208	220	32	608	245632	491264
253	263	197	207	33	627	253308	506616

SOURCE: Reprinted by permission from 3330 Series Disk Storage Reference Summary (Second Edition, November 1973, GX20-1920-1). Copyright 1973 by International Business Machines Corporation.

176

Capacity Table (Contd)

Bytes Per Record				Records Per			
Without Keys		With Keys				3336 Model 1	3336 Model 11
Min	Max	Min	Max	Trk	Cylinder	Pack	Pack
242	252	186	196	34	646	260984	521968
231	241	175	185	35	665	268660	537320
221	230	165	174	36	684	276336	552672
212	220	156	164	37	703	284012	568024
203	211	147	155	38	722	291688	583376
195	202	139	146	39	741	299364	598728
187	194	131	138	40	760	307040	614080
179	186	123	130	41	779	314716	629432
172	178	116	122	42	798	322392	644784
165	171	109	115	43	817	330068	660136
158	164	102	108	44	836	337744	675488
152	157	96	101	45	855	345420	690840
146	151	90	95	46	874	353096	706192
140	145	84	89	47	893	360772	721544
134	139	78	83	48	912	368448	736896
129	133	73	77	49	931	376124	752248
124	128	68	72	50	950	383800	767600
119	123	63	67	51	969	391476	782952
114	118	58	62	52	988	399152	798304
109	113	53	57	53	1007	406828	813656
105	108	49	52	54	1026	414504	829008
101	104	45	48	55	1045	422180	844360
96	100	40	44	56	1064	429856	859712
92	95	36	39	57	1083	437532	875064
89	91	33	35	58	1102	445208	890416
85	88	29	32	59	1121	452884	905768
81	84	25	28	60	1140	460560	921120
78	80	22	24	61	1159	468236	936472
74	77	18	21	62	1178	475912	951824
71	73	15	17	63	1197	483588	967176
68	70	12	14	64	1216	491264	982528
65	67	9	11	65	1235	498940	997880
62	64	6	8	66	1254	506616	1013232
59	61	3	5	67	1273	514292	1028584
56	58	2	2	68	1292	521968	1043936
54	55			69	1311	529644	1059288
51	53			70	1330	537320	1074640
48	50			71	1349	544996	1089992
46	47			72	1368	552672	1105344
43	45			73	1387	560348	1120696
41	42			74	1406	568024	1136048
39	40			75	1425	575700	1151400
36	38			76	1444	583376	1166752
34	35			77	1463	591052	1182104
32	33			78	1482	598728	1197456
30	31			79	1501	606404	1212808
28	29			80	1520	614080	1228160
26	27			81	1539	621756	1243512
24	25			82	1558	629432	1258864
22	23			83	1577	637108	1274216
20	21			84	1596	644784	1289568
19	19			85	1615	652460	1304920

Continued on the following page

Capacity Table (Contd)

Bytes Per Record						Records Per		
Without Keys		With Keys					3336 Model 1	3336 Model 11
Min	Max	Min	Max	Trk	Cylinder	Pack	Pack
17	18			86	1634	660136	1320272
15	16			87	1653	667812	1335624
13	14			88	1672	675488	1350976
12	12			89	1691	683164	1366328
10	11			90	1710	690840	1381680
9	9			91	1729	698516	1397032
7	8			92	1748	706192	1412384
6	6			93	1767	713868	1427736
4	5			94	1786	721544	1443088
3	3			95	1805	729220	1458440
1	2			96	1824	736896	1473792

Speed and Capacity

Access times:

Cylinder to cylinder . . . . 10 milliseconds

Average (entire pack) . . . . 30 milliseconds

Maximum . . . . 55 milliseconds

Data rate:

806 kilobytes per second (1.24 microseconds
per byte)

Rotational delay:

Minimum . . . . 0 milliseconds

Average . . . . 8.4 milliseconds

Maximum . . . . 16.7 milliseconds

Capacity:

	3336 Model 1 Disk Pack*	3336 Model 11 Disk Pack**
Cylinders per pack	404 (plus 7 alternates)	808 (Plus 7 alternates)
Tracks per cylinder	19	19
Tracks per pack	7,809 (including 133 alternates)	15,485 (including 133 alternates)
Track capacity (bytes)	13,030	13,030
Cylinder capacity (bytes)	247,570	247,570
Pack capacity (approx. bytes)	100 million	200 million

*Used with 3330 Series Models 1 or 2
**Used with 3330 Series Model 11

Track Capacity

The number of records that can be recorded on a track depends on the record size. The following equation is used to determine the number of equal-length records per track. Home address and R0 space are accounted for by the equation and the capacity table.

$$\text{Number of equal-length records per track} = \frac{13,165 \quad (\text{track capacity})}{135 + C + KL + DL \quad (\text{bytes per record})}$$

where: KL = key length
DL = data length
C = 0 when $KL = 0$
C = 56 when $KL \neq 0$

Appendix C:

IBM Operating Systems Development

IBM has followed two separate paths of operating systems development. One of these evolutionary paths has produced operating systems for smaller 360 and 370 Series mainframes. The other has provided systems for the larger mainframes of these series of computers. These two parallel lines of operating systems development

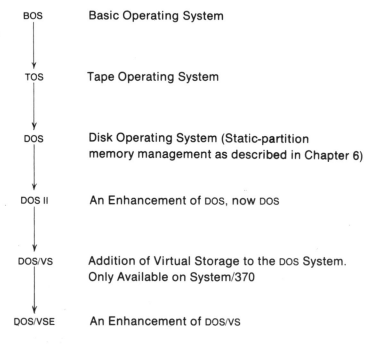

BOS — Basic Operating System

TOS — Tape Operating System

DOS — Disk Operating System (Static-partition memory management as described in Chapter 6)

DOS II — An Enhancement of DOS, now DOS

DOS/VS — Addition of Virtual Storage to the DOS System. Only Available on System/370

DOS/VSE — An Enhancement of DOS/VS

Figure C.1 IBM SMALL MAINFRAME OPERATING SYSTEMS DEVELOPMENT.

180

are pictured in Figures C.1 and C.2, respectively. Note that the virtual storage (VS) systems are those currently marketed. They are available on System/370 only.

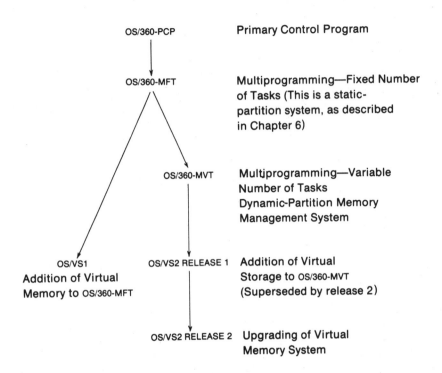

Figure C.2 IBM LARGE MAINFRAME OPERATING SYSTEMS
DEVELOPMENT.

Bibliography

The following topical index is provided for those readers who wish to locate further information on particular subjects. This topical index lists authors' last names for the relevant sources and a number key (in parentheses) to the annotated bibliography.

The annotated bibliography contains selected sources relevant to the material discussed in this book. Many of these sources presume little or no familiarity with computer science or programming. The level of difficulty is noted in most annotations.

Topical Index

184

Selective Annotated
Bibliography

1. *American Society for Information Science Bulletin, 5*(5):entire issue, June 1979.

     This special issue contains several articles discussing the present and future states of the major on-line library networks.
2. Aronofsky, J. S., and Korfhage, R. R. "Telecommunications in Library Networks: A Five-Year Projection." *Journal of Library Automation, 10*(1): 5–27, March 1977.

     This paper outlines the relationship between the growth of telecommunications and library networks and includes predictions concerning the future of this relationship.
3. Avram, H. D. "Toward a Nationwide Library Network." *Journal of Library Automation, 11*(4):285–298, December 1978.

     A view of the Library of Congress's role in the development of a single, nationwide library network.
4. Avram, H., and Droz, J. R. "MARC II and COBOL." *Journal of Library Automation, 1*(4):261–272, December 1968.

     Describes the use of COBOL with machine-readable cataloging records.
5. Boonham, J. C. *Small Systems Computer Sourcebook.* New York, Rococo Press, 1978.

     This book is one of the several generally oriented sourcebooks presently available on microcomputers. It is particularly useful for its lists of hardware and software vendors.
6. Bromberg, H. "The Consequences of Minicomputers." *Datamation, 24*(15): 98–103, November 15, 1978.

     A brief introductory article on minicomputers. Describes what they are, their characteristics, and implications concerning their use.
7. Brooks, E. P. *The Mythical Man-Month: Essays on Software Engineering.* Reading, Mass., Addison-Wesley, 1975.

     The former director of the programming project that created IBM's OS/MVT operating system in the mid-1960s comments on the common pitfalls encountered in large computer projects. Although it is written specifically about projects larger than most libraries attempt, much of what is said about delays, cost overruns, documentation, planning, and project management is pertinent to projects of any size or kind.

8. Brophy, P. *COBOL Programming: An Introduction for Librarians.* Hamden, Conn., Linnet, 1976.

This is a good introductory book on the COBOL programming language. In spite of its title, however, the book is not particularly oriented towards librarians.

9. Chapin, N. *Computers: A Systems Approach.* New York, Van Nostrand, 1971.

This 700-page book covers all aspects of computing systems. Includes a highly specific index.

10. Condon, R. J. *Data Processing: Systems Analysis and Design.* Reston, Va., Reston Publishing, 1975.

A very basic text on systems analysis and design that almost anyone will find useful. It provides an especially good introduction to systems design approaches and logical tools for systems design, including flowcharting, PERT charts, forms design, and Gantt charts. Chapters on hardware and documentation are directly relevant to those topics as presented in this book.

11. Corbato, F. J. "PL/1 as a Tool for Systems Programming." *Datamation,* *15*(5):68–76, May 1969.

This paper discusses advantages and drawbacks concerning the use of PL/1 for systems programming.

12. Dahl, O. J.; Dijkstra, E. W.; and Hoare, C. A. R. *Structured Programming.* London, Academic Press, 1972.

Defines and explains structured programming for programmers.

13. Daiute, R. J., and Gorman, K. A. *Library Operations Research: Computer Programming of Circulation.* Dobbs Ferry, N.Y., Oceana, 1974.

A useful work on the use of computers in library operations research.

14. *Datamation, 24*(8), August 1978.

This special issue features numerous articles on microcomputers. In general, *Datamation* is one of the most relevant and authoritative magazines for computer-system managers and personnel. It includes both news and feature articles.

15. Davis, C. H. "Computer Programming for Librarians." *Journal of Education for Librarianship, 18*(1):41–52, Summer 1977.

Describes experiences in teaching PL/1 to library school students. Includes brief characterizations of programming languages for library use.

16. Davis, C. H. *Illustrative Computer Programming for Libraries: Selected Examples for Information Specialists.* Westport, Conn., Greenwood Press, 1974.

An introductory PL/1 book for librarians. It is particularly worthwhile in that its examples are realistic library programs.

17. Dewar, R. B. K. "SPITBOL Version 2.0 in *SNOBOL4 Project Document S4D23.*" Chicago, Illinois Institute of Technology, 1971. (Informally published manual)

This manual is included in the bibliography because it represents the only source available on the SPITBOL compiler variant of SNOBOL. The use of this manual requires programming background.

18. "Doll on the Evolution of SNA." *Datamation, 26*(3):135–138, March 1980.

    This article provides a brief, semitechnical overview of IBM's networking software, Systems Network Architecture (SNA).

19. Dranov, P. *Automated Library Circulation Systems, 1977–1978.* White Plains, N. Y., Knowledge Industry Publications, 1978.

    This book provides the best and most current overview of the various computerized circulation systems. Several of these circulation systems use minicomputers.

20. Eyre, J., and Tonks, P. *Computers and Systems: An Introduction for Librarians.* London, Clive Bingley, 1971.

    Covers many of the same topics that are discussed in this book. Particularly strong on library systems design.

21. Farber, D. J.; Griswold, R. E.; and Polonsky, I. P. "SNOBOL, a String Manipulation Language." *Journal of the Association for Computing Machinery, 11*(2):21–30, January 1964.

    An overview of the SNOBOL programming language.

22. Flores, I. *Assemblers and BAL.* Englewood Cliffs, N. J., Prentice-Hall, 1971.

    Assembler languages are a highly technical subject, but readers interested in assemblers may find the first few pages of this book informative.

23. Fosdick, H. "Library Education in Information Science: Present Trends." *Special Libraries, 69*(3):100–108, May 1978.

    Discusses trends in information science in library school education. Gives specific recommendations for improvement of current curricula in this area.

24. _____. "The Microcomputer Revolution." *Library Journal, 105*(13): 1467–1472, July 1980.

    An introduction to microcomputers for librarians.

25. _____. "Opting for PL/1: The Strengths of PL/1 Offset the Weaknesses of COBOL." *Computerworld, 14*(32):27–30, August 11, 1980.

    This article compares and contrasts PL/1 and COBOL and includes commentary on the string-manipulation features of the two languages.

26. _____. "Programming Languages for Libraries and Information Centers: An Appraisal and Considerations." *Illinois Libraries, 61*(1):18–25, January 1979.

    This paper discusses the relationship between library programming needs and programming languages in terms similar to those of Chapter 8. Its bibliography includes 40 language-manual references not cited in this bibliography.

27. _____. "An SDC-Based On-Line Search Service." *Special Libraries, 68* (9):305–312, September 1977.

    Presents results and implications of a survey of patron reaction to an SDC-based on-line search service at a small engineering library. Included here for its 35 recent references on on-line search systems.

28. Gilb, T., and Weinberg, G. M. *Humanized Input: Techniques for Reliable Keyed Input.* Cambridge, Mass., Winthrop, 1977.

This work discusses various advanced techniques of data entry into computer files.

29. Gildersleeve, T. R. *Successful Data Processing Systems Analysis.* Englewood Cliffs, N. J., Prentice-Hall, 1978.

A new introductory book on systems analysis. Sections are entitled: Data Collection, Communication, Functional Specifications, and Other Skills.

30. Griswold, R. E. *String and List Processing in SNOBOL4: Techniques and Applications.* Englewood Cliffs, N. J., Prentice-Hall, 1974.

Discussion of the full capabilities of SNOBOL for string processing. Illustrates information retrieval applications. For programmers only.

31. Griswold, R. E., and Griswold, M. T. *A SNOBOL4 Primer.* Englewood Cliffs, N. J., Prentice-Hall, 1973.

The most introductory of all the books on SNOBOL, oriented toward nonprogrammers. A worthwhile book for librarians and library science students.

32. Griswold, R. E.; Poage, J. E.; and Polonsky, I. P. *The SNOBOL4 Programming Language.* Englewood Cliffs, N. J., Prentice-Hall, 1971.

Complete SNOBOL language description for programmers.

33. Grosch, A. N. "Fourth Generation Systems for Libraries: the Marriage of Data Base Management Systems and On-Line Minicomputer Hardware." *Special Libraries,* 68(7 and 8):221–227, July/August 1977.

This paper discusses two of the most important new technologies in computer science and their probable impacts on libraries.

34. _____. *Minicomputers in Libraries, 1979–1980.* White Plains, N. Y., Knowledge Industry Publications, 1979.

This booklet provides an up-to-date view of minicomputer use in libraries.

35. Hayes, R. M., and Becker, J. *Handbook of Data Processing for Libraries.* New York, Wiley, 1970.

Most librarians interested in automation are already familiar with this 900-page sourcebook of information on library data processing. Appendixes include a bibliography, a glossary of terms, and a list of journal sources on data processing in the library.

36. Heilinger, E. M., and Henderson, P. B. *Library Automation: Experience, Methodology and Technology of the Library as an Information System.* New York, McGraw-Hill, 1971.

This book includes sections on the methodology of library automation, computer hardware, and software concepts associated with the library use of computers.

37. Hopkins, M. "Problems of PL/1 for Systems Programming." In: IBM, Research Report RC 3489. Yorktown Heights, N.Y., IBM, August 5, 1971.

Discusses difficulties in using PL/1 for systems programming.

38. Hume, J. N. P., and Holt, R. C. *Structured Programming Using PL/1 and SP/k.* Reston, Va., Reston Publishing, 1975.

This introductory textbook on PL/1 is listed here for two of its chapters, "Alphabetic Information Handling" and "The Computer Can Read English." These chapters are particularly relevant to the topic of string handling in PL/1.

39. IBM Corporation. *Introduction to IBM Data Processing Systems.* Poughkeepsie, N.Y., IBM Publications Services, 1970.

    A general work on data-processing systems, distributed by IBM as a student text. It covers some of the subjects discussed in this book: storage devices, I/O devices, general hardware concepts, programming languages, and operating systems.

40. IBM Data Processing Division. *System/7-2790 Library Circulation Control.* White Plains, N. Y., IBM Data Processing Division, 1973.

    This brief booklet describes a minicomputer circulation system developed by IBM for libraries in the early 1970s.

41. IEEE. *Sixth Data Communications Symposium.* New York, Institute of Electrical and Electronics Engineers, 1979.

    This technical work provides state-of-the-art information concerning recent developments in computer networking.

42. Johnson, M. F. "A Design for a Minicomputer Based Serials Control Network." *Special Libraries, 67*(7):386–390, August 1976.

    Serials control through a minicomputer network is the topic of this paper.

43. *Journal of Library Automation, 10*(2):entire issue, June 1977.

    This issue of *JOLA* was devoted to networking. Special emphasis is accorded the topic of the institutional cooperation that must underlie any attempt at computer networking.

44. Kapp, D., and Leban, J. F. *IMS Programming Techniques: A Guide to Using DL/I.* New York, Van Nostrand Reinhold, 1978, pp.1–17.

    The first 20 pages of this book describe the purposes of database organization, the IBM family of IMS systems, and hierarchical organization principles. The remainder is a technical programmer's guide and is probably of little interest here.

45. Kimber, R. T. *Automation in Libraries.* New York, Pergamon Press, 1974.

    This book on library automation discusses in each chapter the different functional subsystems found in libraries.

46. King, W. R., and Wilson, T. A. "Subjective Time Estimates in Critical Path Planning." *Management Science, 13*(5):307–320, January 1967.

47. King, W. R.; Witterrongel, D. M.; and Hezel, K. D. "On the Analysis of Critical Path Time Estimating Behavior." *Management Science, 14*(1):79–84, September 1967.

48. Lancaster, F. W., ed. *Proceedings of the 1974 Clinic on Library Applications of Data Processing: Applications of Minicomputers to Library and Related Problems.* Urbana-Champaign, University of Illinois, 1974.

    A compilation of papers on experiences concerning minicomputer use in library automation projects, this book is an excellent source on minicomputer systems in libraries. Also includes a contribution on the use of a database system at the University of Chicago. Other recent books in this series also may be of interest, most notably the following: 1975—*The Use of Computers in Literature Searching and Related Reference Activities in Libraries;* 1973—*Networking and Other Forms of Cooperation;* 1972—*Applications of On-line Computers to Library Problems.* The last includes papers from 1972 on LOLITA, BALLOTS, and the Ohio State University and Northwestern University on-line circulation systems.

49. *LARC Series on Automated Activities in Health Science Libraries, 1*(2):entire issue, 1975.

   This issue treats on-line systems in special libraries.

50. Libbey, M. A. "Very High Programming Languages (e.g., SNOBOL, COMIT) in the Special Librarian's Future." *Special Libraries, 66*(8): 363–366, August 1975.

   A discussion of SNOBOL and COMIT for library programming.

51. Liebowitz, B. H., and Carson, J. H., eds. *Distributed Processing.* 2nd Edition. New York, Institute of Electrical and Electronics Engineers, 1978.

   This computer science tutorial provides an introduction to many of the software aspects of computer networking.

52. Link, J. D. *Handbook of Microprocessors, Microcomputers, and Minicomputers.* Englewood Cliffs, N.J., Prentice-Hall, 1979.

   A very complete and nontechnical introduction to microcomputers.

53. Little, J. L. "A Computer Network Protocol at the Application Level for Libraries and Other Information Science Services." *Journal of Library Automation, 11*(3):239–245, September 1978.

   This paper describes protocols for computer networking among libraries.

54. London, K. R. *Documentation Standards.* New York, Petrocelli Books, 1974.

   A definitive work on all aspects of documentation. Documentation is treated according to the same categories used in Chapter 9 of this book.

55. MacCafferty, M. *An Annotated Bibliography of Automation in Libraries and Information Systems 1972-1975.* London, Aslib, 1976.

   A well-indexed bibliography of sources in this area.

56. Martin, S. K. *Library Networks, 1978-1979.* White Plains, N.Y., Knowledge Industry Publications, 1978.

   This is one of the best current sources of information concerning library networks, because it discusses all major topics concerning them.

57. Martin, S. K., and Butler, B., eds. *Library Automation: The State of the Art II.* Chicago, American Library Association, 1975.

   Papers from an ALA Institute on Library Automation held in 1973. The discussion is structured according to the various functional subsystems automated in the library.

58. Matthews, S. E. "Operation and Cost of Running Library Circulation On-Line with System/7-2790." *Illinois Libraries, 61*(1):31–49, January 1979.

   Costs and other aspects of an experience with an on-line minicomputer circulation system are explored in this paper.

59. Metzger, P. W. *Managing a Programming Project.* Englewood Cliffs, N. J., Prentice-Hall, 1973.

Systems development projects are divided into six distinct phases, and all aspects of project development are discussed within this context. Outlines are given for the major documents produced during a project. Extremely useful for analysts and administrators involved in or contemplating a programming or automation project.

60. Milner, R. "String Handling in ALGOL." *Computer Journal, 10*(4):321–424, February 1968.

The main source for string manipulation in ALGOL.

61. Mott, T. H.; Artandi, S.; and Struminger, L. *Introduction to PL/1 Programming for Library and Information Science.* New York, Academic Press, 1972.

A longer, more complete, and more ambitious guide to PL/I for librarians than C. H. Davis's book.

62. North, S. "The ABC's of Microcomputers." *Creative Computing, 4*(2):89–91, March–April 1978.

A brief and general article on microcomputers. *Creative Computing* is a major journal for information on microcomputer hardware and software.

63. Orilia, L. S.; Stern, N. B.; and Stern, R. A. *Business Data Processing Systems.* 2nd Edition. New York, Wiley, 1977.

Covers the logical tools of systems design and forms design as well.

64. Palmer, R. P. *Case Studies in Library Computer Systems.* New York, R. R. Bowker, 1973.

Case studies in library automation as of 1973. Includes projects that failed as well as the successes.

65. Philappakis, A. S. "A Popularity Contest for Languages." *Datamation, 23* (12):81–87, December 1977.

Recent data on the popularity of individual programming languages in nationwide data-processing use.

66. Saffady, W. "String Processing Facilities of Programming Languages." *Special Libraries, 67*(9):415–420, September 1976.

Describes and evaluates various programming languages in relation to their string-processing capabilities.

67. Salmon, S. R. *Library Automation Systems.* New York, Marcel Dekker, 1975.

This handbook discusses specific library automation experiences.

68. Salton, G. "Suggestions for Library Network Design." *Journal of Library Automation, 12*(1):39–52, March 1979.

This paper provides a conceptual overview of certain principles relevant to the design of library computer networks.

69. Sammet, J. E. *Programming Languages: History and Fundamentals.* Englewood Cliffs, N.J., Prentice-Hall, 1969.

A classic work that describes all programming languages, their characteristics, and historical development. Worthwhile for those with and without programming background.

70. Sanderson, P. C. *Minicomputers.* London, Newnes-Butterworths, 1976.

This thin volume offers an introductory and complete look at minicomputers from a British viewpoint. Chapters include: Selecting the Minicomputer System, Software, Programming, and Applications. Some sections are technical.

71. Schossberg, E.; Brockman, J.; and Horton, L. *Home Computer Handbook.* New York, Sterling Publishing, 1978.

Oriented toward the home computing market, this book provides a nontechnical introduction to microcomputers.

72. Semprevivo, P. C. *Systems Analysis: Definition, Process and Design.* Chicago, Science Research Associates, 1976. This textbook discusses systems design tools, data collection, and project planning.

73. Silverston, S. M. *SNOBAT 1.9: A Processor for SNOBOL4.* Ames, Computation Center at Iowa State University, 1976.

The manual for the SNOBAT compiler version of SNOBOL. For programmers only.

74. Smith, G. L., and Meyer, R. S., eds. *Library Use of Computers: An Introduction.* New York, Special Libraries Association, 1969.

Useful source for introductory discussions of various computing concepts. Written specifically for librarians.

75. Swihart, S. J., and Beryl, F. H. *Computer Systems in the Library: A Handbook for Managers and Designers.* Los Angeles, Melville, 1973.

A complete handbook for administrators and directors of library automation projects.

76. Tedd, L. A. *An Introduction to Computer-Based Library Systems.* London, Heyden and Sons, 1977.

A student text of broad scope, covering library automation subsystems to SDI, computer-produced indexes, and retrospective search systems.

77. Tharp, A. L. *Applications of SPITBOL.* Raleigh, North Carolina State University, 1977.

Library programmers and researchers will be especially interested in the information retrieval programming examples contained in this book. The book also contains other text-processing examples of relevance to libraries.

78. Yngve, V. H. "COMIT." *Communications of the Association for Computing Machinery,* 6(1):83–84, January 1963.

Short introductory description of the COMIT programming language for those with programming backgrounds.

79. _____. "COMIT as an Information Retrieval Language." *Communications of the Association for Computing Machinery,* 5(1):19–28, January 1972.

This paper is particularly important to librarianship because it discusses the relevance of COMIT for information retrieval programming.

80. _____. *Computer Programming with COMIT II.* Cambridge, Mass., MIT Press, 1972.

The most complete work on COMIT II.

81. Young, M. J.; Pessanite, F. A.; and Reisinger, J. C. *Introduction to Mini-computers in Federal Libraries*. Washington, D.C., Library of Congress, 1978.

   A complete overview of federal libraries' use of minicomputing systems.

Index

Abnormal termination, 78
Access method, *See also* individual
    access methods by name
    48, 108, 111–113
Access time, 30, 60–64, 72, 112
ADABAS database system, 151, 159
Address, 86–87, 97
Address space, 87, 96–97, 99
Addressability, 86–87, 96–97
American Standard Code for
    Information Interchange (ASCII),
    8–12, 33, 52, Appendix A
Analyst, *See* Systems analyst
Applications programmer, *See also*
    Programmer
    17, 24–26, 83–84
Arithmetic/logical unit, 3–4
Arithmetic operation, 3–4
ASCII, *See* American Standard Code
    for Information Interchange
Assembly language, 120–125, 131

Backup copies, 66
Base relocation register, *See*
    Relocation register
Base two arithmetic, *See* Binary
    numbers
BASIC, *See* Beginners All-purpose
    Symbolic Instruction Code
Basic access method, 111
Basic Direct Access Method (BDAM),
    112
Basic Sequential Access Method
    (BSAM), 112

Basic Telecommunications Access
    Method (BTAM), 115
BCD, *See* Binary Coded Decimal
BDAM, *See* Basic Direct Access
    Method
BDW, *See* Block descriptor word
Beginners All-purpose Symbolic In-
    struction Code (BASIC), 130, 168
Bibliographic citation retrieval
    systems, 146
Bibliographic Retrieval Services, Inc.
    (BRS), 146
Bifurcate, 127
Binary Coded Decimal (BCD), 8, 52
Binary digit, *See* Bit
Binary mathematics, *See* Binary
    numbers
Binary numbers, 9–12
Bit, 7–12
Block descriptor word (BDW),
    38–39, 50
Blocking/deblocking, *See also* Disk,
    example calculations with;
    Tape, example calculations
    with
    45–50, 60–61, 111
Blocking factor, *See also* Disk,
    example calculations with; Tape,
    example calculations with
    46–47, 60–61
Blocksize, *See also* Disk, example
    calculations with; Tape,
    example calculations with
    46–47

197